Stories of a Paratrooper in Occupied Japan

PFC Hansen of the 11th Airborne Division,
a Clerk and Paratrooper in Sendai, Japan,
in 1946-47 after WWII

Written by

Norman R. Hansen

Edited by

Barry W. Hansen

Barry Hansen
Jan 2019

Mostly stories, with a good bit of travel, troop ships,
training, paratrooping and Japan.

Barry W. Hansen

17050 Hamlin Rd NE

Lake Forest Park, Washington 98155

E-mail: barry.hansen@gmail.com

Website: www.normanrhansen.com

First Edition, 2018

ISBN-13: 978-1536916072

ISBN-10: 1536916072

Cover

Front cover:

Norman is one of a few Army soldiers to ride on the Navy's new *USS Hollister* during a shake-down cruise from Sendai to Aomori. Story on page 83.

Back cover:

Downtown Sendai with street vendors and storefronts on both sides with trolley tracks down the middle. Page 140.

Norman at his desk holding Daisy in his lap. He's supposed to be studying an algebra correspondence course and instead puts his glasses on Daisy.
Read "Office Life" on page 61.

Parachute Type T-7 is the chute everyone used in paratrooper jump school. This diagram is reproduced from 1947 handouts. See "Paratrooper Jump School" on page 35.

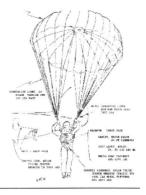

Norman visited a park near Sendai and met these children wearing a traditional outfit and sandals.

Read "Stroll in the Park" on page 144.

C-46 Curtiss Commando being refueled on the runway at Carelus Field at Yamoto.

See "Jump Preparation" on page 37.

Sincere thanks to my proofreaders Janelle Retka in Phnom Penh, Cambodia and Vicki Stiles of Shoreline Historical Museum, Seattle. All remaining errors are my own.

Cover design by Vladimir Verano, Third Place Books, Lake Forest Park, Washington, USA.

Table of Contents

About the Authors

1946 — Norman Hansen, 19, at the army base in Sendai, Japan

Norman Hansen was a widower and retired Shoreline School District elementary school teacher. He lived in Washington State throughout his long life. Norm was raised in Richmond Beach in the city of Shoreline. He settled on five acres in Bellevue, then one acre with horses in Kirkland and finally moved to a half-acre in Lake Forest Park in 1973. He retired in 1985 and passed away August 17, 2016 after writing and reviewing this book.

Barry Hansen was born in Bellevue and raised in Kirkland, earned his Electrical Engineering degree from Washington State University and worked as a design engineer for IBM in Minnesota for twelve years. Over the years, he advanced through a series of progressively smaller software companies including Attachmate and WRQ until he worked for himself in Sammamish, Washington, running his own web design business. He now owns what was Norman's property and retired in Lake Forest Park in 2017. He enjoys amateur radio with call sign K7BWH.

2016 — Norman Hansen, 88, (left) with his son Barry, 60

Books by the Authors

- *Stories of a Paratrooper in Occupied Japan: PFC Hansen of the 11th Airborne Division, a Clerk and Paratrooper in Sendai, Japan, in 1946-47 after WWII.* Written by Norman R. Hansen and edited by Barry W. Hansen, ©2018, ISBN 978-1536916072

- *Stories of Richmond Beach: Memories and Photos of Small-Town Life on Puget Sound in the 1930s-1940s.* Written by Norman R. Hansen and edited by Barry W. Hansen, ©2015, ISBN 978-1502382597

- *Autumn Tango: Pony Club Outlaw.* Written by Winifred M. Hansen and edited by Barry W. Hansen, ©2016, ISBN 978-1515141501

- www.NormanRHansen.com, a companion website for these books.

Dedication

This book is for my children, grandchildren and great-grandchildren for the love I have for them and the love they express to me.

At the time of writing in the summer of 2016, I have three children, nine grandchildren and ten great-grandchildren. I dedicate this book to my wonderful extended family. I hope they grow up to explore the world, try new experiences and remember everything.

My three children:

> Kurt (deceased), Carol, Barry

My nine grandchildren:

> Kurt: Jennifer, Aimé, Ryan, Brandon
> Carol: Benjamin, Anna
> Barry: Hillary, Tyler, Daryl

My ten great-grandchildren:

> Jennifer: Madeline, Keegan
> Aimé: Jaiden, Ethan
> Ryan: Spencer, Ashton, Ryan
> Benjamin: Dominic, Jadyn, Jonathan

Norman R. Hansen

Foreword

This book has been fifteen years in the making. It began from conversations in hotel rooms. My son Barry then started making voice recordings in the evenings during our cross-country drive from Seattle to Terre Haute, Indiana, in August 2003. Over the years, Barry encouraged me to tell and write more stories while he transcribed everything into a good collection of notes. When we discovered the rolls of original negatives from my assignment in Japan, he scanned them, and those photos triggered more recollections and stories. Then we found my old army newsletter archives and my printed material from Japan, which helped me generate even more stories and construct a more detailed timeline.

Somewhat to my surprise, this collection turned into a significant body of material. In 2016, Barry and I worked closely together to flesh out the stories, add pictures, polish the writing, organize the stories into themes and reformat the manuscript for publishing. We worked diligently on this while I received cancer treatments and Barry was living with me.

I hope you enjoy these stories about my life as an army paratrooper in occupied Japan after World War II in 1946 to 47. It is written mostly from memory and from my photographs taken at the time. Undoubtedly, errors of fact or recollection will have crept into this book, for which I take full responsibility.

Author's Introduction

I am the middle of Rollin and Leone Hansen's five children. Born in Seattle in September 1927, just prior to the Great Depression, I grew up in Richmond Beach, Washington, with my two parents, three brothers and a sister. My parents raised us in the "little house" built by my father in 1925 on property owned by—and a few feet from—my great-grandfather, Morton Anderson, and his "big house." When I was a teenager, we moved to the "big house"—the one built by Morton in 1902.

September 1935 — Norman, 8, in the middle of his family line-up. The homemade clothing has a Pop Eye cartoon patch on the boys' pantleg. Left to right: Merna, Roald, Norman, Donald and Robert

In many ways, it was not an easy life for our family. Rollin worked as a laborer, a carpenter's helper and also on a Norwegian neighbor's fishing boat. He then went to work for Standard Oil at Point Wells as a longshoreman for many years. Our family got by because of a large garden, chickens, pigs, a couple of milk cows and a lot of hard work. Leone sewed much of the children's clothing. Although money was scarce, we had plenty of food, music, cooperation and fun.

September 24, 1944 — Norman, 17, at their home in Richmond Beach. Leone took many photos with the family arranged by age. Left to right: Rollin, Leone, Merna, Roald, Norman, Donald and Robert

I graduated from Richmond Beach High School in 1945 and was elected Student Body President that year. Though not particularly athletic, I did earn a letter in football in my junior and senior years. I earned enough credits to graduate in February 1945 instead of in June with the rest of my high school classmates.

My goal was to get a college degree, but first I needed to accumulate savings to pay for it. So, I took a job with Standard Oil and set aside most of my paycheck for college expenses. My job continued from February through August 1945, when I enrolled for a semester at the University of Washington in Seattle. I was commuting daily from our family home in Richmond Beach to the university, a trip of about forty-five minutes, by riding with friends or taking the bus. I chose journalism as my major since I had enjoyed my time as the high school newspaper editor in my junior year.

*Summer 1945 — Norman, 17, developed muscles after a
summer of long days and hard work for Standard Oil*

It was not long before I became acutely aware that choosing journalism for my major was a major mistake (pun intended). I had entered the University of Washington in September of 1945, coming from a school with less than one hundred high school students and went to a university with 17,000 students, many of them serious adult World War II veterans. This was an unpleasant culture shock.

Needless to say, though I tried hard and passed all my courses, the result was nothing to brag about. However, as you will soon see, this short experience gave me unexpected opportunities that shaped my entire army career.

End of WWII

"Occupied Japan" refers to the six or seven years after World War II from 1945 through April 1952. It was during this time that the allies "occupied" Japan.

Bombing of Sendai

September 18, 1945 — Sendai after a massive Allied air raid.
Image from Wikipedia. Photographer is not known.

The city of Sendai, host to the largest population and the commercial center of the Tohoku region of northern Honshu Island, was heavily bombed by the U.S. in July 1945 as part of strategic bombing campaigns against the civilian population and military targets during the closing stages of World War II.

To get a sense of the massive scale involved, consider this: 123 Allied aircraft arrived over this target at an altitude of 10,000 feet after midnight of July 20, 1945. The bombers split into twenty-five groups of between two and five aircraft each to carpet-bomb the densely packed residential center of the city with 10,961 incendiary bombs.

The resultant firestorm destroyed most of the historic center of the city. As a result of this one attack, 2,755 civilians were killed and 57,321 were injured (approximately 26 percent of the population at the time). Five square kilometers of the city center were totally destroyed and nearly 12,000 residences burned (approximately 23 percent of the city).

Surrender

Japan surrendered to the allies on August 14, 1945. On the following day, Emperor Hirohito announced Japan's unconditional surrender on the radio. This date is known as "Victory Over Japan," or V-J Day, which marked the end of World War II.

On V-J Day, U.S. President Harry Truman appointed General Douglas MacArthur as Supreme Commander for the Allied Powers (SCAP) to supervise the occupation of Japan with support from the British Commonwealth.

Truman approved a document outlining the post-surrender policy for Japan with two main objectives for the occupation: (1) eliminating Japan's war potential, and (2) turning Japan into a Western-style nation with a pro-American orientation.

This period was a time of great change in Japan. For example, the Shinto Directive, issued on December 15, 1945, abolished Shinto as a state religion and prohibited some of its teachings and rites that were deemed to be militaristic or ultra-nationalistic. In 1947, the new Constitution of Japan enfranchised women, guaranteed fundamental human rights, strengthened the powers of Parliament and the Cabinet, and decentralized the police and local government. In 1946, the Japanese writing system was drastically reorganized by the *tōyō kanji*—a standardized list of characters (a predecessor of today's *jōyō kanji*)—and by greatly altering orthography to reflect spoken usage.

Today, in 2016, we often complain about the rapid rate of change in our American society. I can't imagine how much greater the broad transformations must have felt in Japan back then. Most of their government, religion, commerce, language and more were suddenly subjected to radical change.

Occupation

Allied forces, primarily American, were set up to supervise the country following its surrender in 1945. The occupation ultimately lasted almost seven years.

General MacArthur's first priority was to set up a food distribution network; following the collapse of the ruling government and the wholesale destruction of most major cities, practically everyone was starving. Even with these measures, millions of people were still on the brink of starvation for several years after the surrender.

Once the food network was in place, MacArthur set out to win the support of Hirohito. The two men met for the first time on September 27; the photograph of the two together is one of the most famous in Japanese history.

September 27, 1945 — Douglas MacArthur and Emperor Hirohito
Photo by Gaetano Faillace

All in all, the occupation of Japan was a truly remarkable feat of logistics and movement of a huge amount of men and materials. By the end of 1945, more than 350,000 U.S. personnel were stationed throughout Japan. By the beginning of 1946, replacement troops began to arrive in the country in large numbers (including me, draftee PFC Norman Hansen) and were assigned to MacArthur's 8th Army. Troop numbers peaked in the summer of 1946 and began slowly decreasing in the fall of 1947 as draftees (including me, again) were replaced by Regular Army troops.

Camp Schimmelpfennig

In September 1945, Camp Schimmelpfennig, the largest base of GHQ north of Tokyo, was set up in Nigatake, Sendai. Camp Schimmelpfennig was built on land previously used as the Japanese arsenal and named after the chief of staff who was killed in combat. This became the Division Headquarters. As you will soon see, I arrived in August 1946, about a year after V-J Day, and Camp Schimmelpfennig was to become my home for the next twelve months.

In 1956, the Camp was renamed Camp Sendai. It is reported that today, in 2016, you can still see the base, less than a ten-minute train ride from Sendai Station. The area is now the site of Kawauchi Campus of Tohoku University, and many of the original camp buildings—hastily constructed with wooden two-by-four architecture—were subsequently demolished when they expanded the university campus.

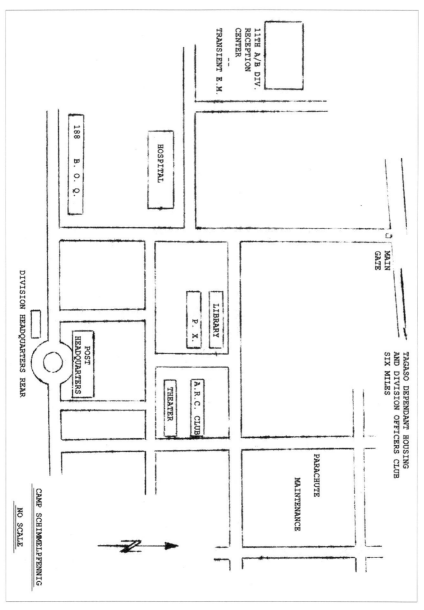

May 12, 1947 – Map of Camp Schimmelpfennig
Reproduced from my handouts

Entering the Army

Early in April 1946, I received a heartfelt letter from my suddenly close and very dear personal friend, President Harry S. Truman:

Order to Report for Induction

From: The President of the United States

Greetings: Having submitted yourself to a Local Board composed of your neighbors for the purpose of determining your availability for training and service in the Armed Forces of the United States, you will therefore report to the Local Board ...

Having therefore presented myself on the date and time as directed, it turned out that my services were required for an indefinite period in the U.S. Army. Thus, on April 19, 1946, I was inducted. There were four of us from the north end of Seattle who made our way to Fort Lewis in Tacoma, Washington. We were given physicals, shots and uniforms. All of my clothing went home, and I was garbed from head to toe in olive drab U.S. Army clothes: shirts, pants, underwear, socks—everything, except for shoes, was olive drab.

After an introduction to army chow and a night in the barracks, we were shipped by train to Fort McClellan, a training center near Anniston, Alabama. One of the country's largest U.S. Army installations, it trained an estimated half-million troops during World War II.

Basic Training in Alabama's hot, humid spring and summer was a bit of a trial, but I was young, fit and eager to prove myself.

Basic Training in Alabama

I had led a very sheltered and conventional life in rural Richmond Beach, Washington, living alongside our extended family and our barnyard animals and large vegetable garden. I was soon to get acquainted with some of the rest of the world. In the army, I encountered people from all over the U.S. with a wide variety of regional accents and cultural backgrounds. It was very educational and, on occasion, very trying.

To be effective, soldiers need to be physically fit. So, of course, basic training included large doses of strength and endurance training. To illustrate the point, at our company's first formation (a regular "Chinese fire drill"), our sergeant ordered us to lift our nine-pound rifles by the barrel and hold them straight out from the shoulder. He did the same with his rifle and he held it there until every man in the company could no longer hold up his rifle. Very impressive.

A number of experiences stand out in my mind. A draftee named John Paul Jones had problems with "left" and "right." This was not an obvious problem until we practiced close order drill with fixed bayonets on rifles over the shoulder. The order given was "column right" and John turned left, his bayonet striking the soldier next to him. The army finally determined that this was an innate problem and Mr. Jones was given a medical discharge. This was long before our modern understanding of the problem of dyslexia. Later in life, I became a schoolteacher and specialized in dyslexia and other learning disabilities.

One of the ways our instructors tried to develop our physical strength and teamwork involved an exercise with a timber log about a foot in diameter and ten or so feet long. Our platoon of eight would line up alongside the log and, on command, pick it up and hold it overhead. Perhaps then we would have to put it down on our other side. This log could go back and forth or be held overhead while marching. It made us terribly hot and sweaty. Any slackers were soon identified and brought up to snuff.

Whenever there was a break in our training, the sergeant would command, "Hit the lean and rest!" This position was a prelude to push-ups. It consisted of being face down, toes on the ground and arms from the shoulder to ground kept straight. It was a sight to see, all of us lined up, backs straight, lowering in unison and pushing back up together. It hurt, but it did build shoulder muscles and core strength.

Personal hygiene was especially important in close quarters and a hot climate. Coming in from such hot, sweaty training in the late afternoon called for a welcome shower. Millard, a farm boy from the Midwest, apparently had never learned the habit. After a couple of days, he had become quite "ripe." An invitation to shower being refused, we simply hauled him to the showers, stripped him and, using harsh brown soap and a stiff scrub brush normally used on floors, left him a rosy pink. The next day it was, "Millard, let's go shower," and he instantly replied, "Be right with you!"

Close order drill was a major part of basic training and we did a lot of it. This form of marching was designed to move large groups of men efficiently and orderly, and to train soldiers to react promptly and together as a unit. Some of the commands we learned were:

Forward, March
Column Right, March
Platoon Halt
To the Rear, March
Double Time, March
My favorite: Double to the Rear by the Right Flank, March!

Strangely enough, these commands seemed rather fun, and during free time at the barracks you might see platoons practicing when they could be resting.

We learned to care for our equipment in great detail. Each of us was issued an M1 rifle, and we were expected to keep it clean at all times. Every company in training would have its rifles collected for inspection at random times. Company C, my company, had the distinction of having every single rifle in the company pass inspection—they were all clean, well-oiled and without any pitting. Apparently, this was a first in the history of the training center. Our captain was very pleased and gave us the afternoon off.

One Thursday, our barracks hiked about two miles to the rifle range to shoot our M1s for marksmanship. A messenger came to inform us that a track meet was planned for the next Saturday and "Did anyone want to try out for track?" Thus, I volunteered to enter the one-mile foot race. This meant packing everything back the two miles and then running a timed mile to qualify. I managed the mile with my best time ever: almost exactly five minutes. Soon came Saturday, it was about 90 degrees and very humid. I was still stiff and sore from Thursday's hiking and time trial. Approximately twenty soldiers started the race, but only seven of us finished, and many of the rest simply collapsed along the way. I was quite pleased to finish in sixth place.

A modern example of a typical 81 mm mortar
Image from Adobe Stock Photo

Another interesting feature of our training was learning to fire an 81 mm mortar. A mortar team consisted three people: one to carry the heavy iron base plate, another to carry the mortar tube, and a third to carry ammunition and to serve as a "spotter." The biggest and strongest soldier usually carried the base plate.

The concept of mortar fire was to lob a mortar round from a hidden area to a target area the mortar team can't see. So, we packed the gear through hilly Alabama pine woods to the base of another hill. The spotter hiked to the top to locate the dummy structures that were our target down in the far valley. The mortar was assembled with a system to measure and set elevation and direction. Our "ammo" was torpedo-shaped with a recess in the base that accepted shotgun shells, but without pellets; the shells were simply to propel the round. Our dummy rounds looked like real ammunition, fins and all. The spotter then relayed directions for setting up the first of five shots such that the "bomb," or round, be in line with the target but fall short of it. Next, one of us would drop a mortar down the tube where the center of the shotgun shell struck a firing pin. Then the spotter, assessing the results of the round, readjusted the aim such that the second mortar round would land approximately as far beyond the target as the first fell short. Observing the result, he would interpolate the difference and call out new settings. Now the command was to "fire three for effect." To balance things out, each of us got to play each role. Aside from the awful weight of the gear and the noise, it was really fun, especially when the spotter did a good job and landed all three rounds on the little wooden target huts.

The term of our service for those of us drafted into the army was "at the pleasure of the President." We, the draftees, were targeted by efforts to get us to sign up for the Regular Army, where the term of enlistment was eighteen months. This was fairly tempting, and when they offered a bonus of $300 (a good amount of money in those days), it became a no-brainer decision. Four of us from the Northwest hatched a clever plan to save or even make more money. We were *sure* we'd be shipped back to Seattle, so we would pool our money, buy a used car, cash a travel chit, drive back home at lower cost than public transportation, sell the car and split the proceeds. So, we were discharged on the morning of May 20, 1946, and almost immediately sworn into the Regular Army.

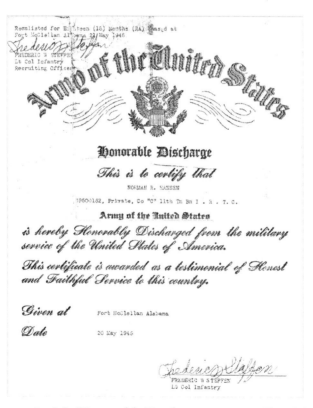

May 20, 1946 – My Honorable Discharge papers at Fort McClellan, Alabama, in preparation to join the Regular Army

Then our clever plan went into the toilet. They sent two of us directly to Germany and two of us to Japan via Puget Sound. Don Robinson and I were put onto a train to Fort Lawton in Seattle. From Alabama north to Chicago, we rode a coal-fired train that seemed to produce a ton of dirty black cinders every mile. Our clothes and skin soon became gritty, and for five days and four nights on a "day coach" we had no place to shower or launder our clothes. How pleasant to switch to diesel in Chicago! At nineteen years of age, in uniform in Chicago, I bought a bottle of whisky—my first ever. Also a first was the train ride through an eight-mile Snoqualmie Tunnel in the Cascade Mountains near Snoqualmie Pass. In modern times the tunnel is part of the Iron Horse State Park near Interstate 90 and is paved and open for pedestrians and cyclists. It makes a cool and refreshing bicycle ride on a hot summer's day and is a trip that Barry has enjoyed.

After the long ordeal on the day coach train, we welcomed the bunks and showers at Fort Lawton. As we were ready to ship out to Japan, there wasn't much to do in camp. So, for the few days we were there, security being lax, I sometimes took the bus home to Richmond Beach, being very certain to be back in camp before bed check.

Fort Lawton was a United States Army post in a portion of Seattle overlooking Puget Sound called the Magnolia neighborhood. Much later, in 1973, this became Discovery Park after a large majority of Fort Lawton (534 acres), was given to the city of Seattle. Both the Fort and the nearby residential neighborhood of Lawton Wood are named after Major General Henry Ware Lawton.

USS Marine Devil

USS Marine Devil, our troop carrier to Japan
Image from C.E. Daniel Collection

Early in August of 1946, the troop ship *USS Marine Devil* departed from Fort Lawton, Seattle, for Yokohama with about 3,000 troops, as far as I can remember. Taking the northern route, which is the shortest distance based on the great circle route, we came within a hundred miles or so from the Aleutian Islands. The trip took fourteen days.

Fort Lawton was a quiet outpost prior to World War II, but suddenly became the second largest port of embarkation of soldiers and material to the Pacific Theater during the war. Fort Lawton officially closed September 14, 2011.

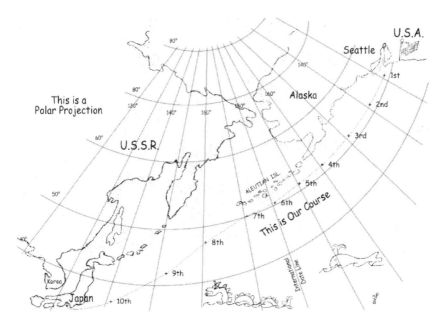

A sketch of our Great Circle route from Ft Lawton to Yokohama Bay

Special Services

Here is one instance in which my brief college experience paid off. The lieutenant in charge of Special Services approached me and invited me to be editor of a daily mimeographed newspaper, "*The Devil's Tale.*" I accepted, of course. I also had two helpers. We had an office with materials including a movie projector and a number of films.

Some wonderful benefits came along with this job. We were issued a pass that put us at the head of any mess hall line. In addition, we were welcome to a last evening snack from leftovers. The fellow in charge gave us a great big stack of 8-by-10 inch photographs of the *USS*

Marine Devil. Well, that was all right with me—we sold them all for fifty cents apiece!

Each day, I was privileged to visit the bridge and collect information such as our progress, location, weather and sport scores—all fodder for our daily "rag." It took most of the day to prepare and print the issues. One of the fellows was a good (read: "fair") artist, so we included cartoons. We made a joint effort to construct simple crossword puzzles. Perhaps this was a trigger that kept me solving crosswords for the rest of my life. In our spare time, we watched films. The Special Services was both a sinecure and valuable learning experience.

A sinecure is, of course, a position requiring little or no work but giving the holder status or financial benefit. Some synonyms are: easy job, cushy job, soft option.

Candy Bars

Shortly before shipping out, I happened to be in the PX (Post Exchange) store in Fort Lawton. On impulse, I bought a box of twenty-four Hershey's candy bars with almonds and tucked them deep into my duffel bag. They were a substantial size, bigger than all of today's bars except the "king sized" big ones. They were a real PX bargain at five cents each.

I had been on board for maybe a week or so when I took one of those bars up on deck and began to unwrap it. Some soldier came up alongside me and asked, "Where did you get *that?*" It seemed that there was no PX on board, and almost 3,000 soldiers had been paid but had nowhere to spend their money. Black-jack, poker games and crap games were rampant on board and some soldiers were quite flush with money. I told him that I brought it with me.

"Well, would you sell it?"

I asked him what he'd give me for it.

"Would you take five dollars?"

I sold that *whole boxful* of five cent candy bars for five dollars each. How sweet it was! My college fund was already growing.

Most of our protective "shots" against oriental diseases were administered at Fort Lawton, but for some reason, the inoculation against Japanese B encephalitis was given on board. This shot was not only painful but also left a lump on one's shoulder that took three days to absorb, while burning all that time. It had better be worth it!

Really, the voyage to Japan was a "pleasure cruise" for me. We were busy, but I didn't have to milk the cows, chop wood or weed the garden. It was a neat trip. We had duties but, of course, the three of us were also having fun. Being in the Special Services was such a good deal.

On board, space was at a premium. Ship bunks were set on poles and vertical space was well-used by stacking them seven bunks high. By happenstance, I found a top bunk that was available. A ladder was alongside the bunk. One big advantage was my location next to a series of ducts which made an excellent storage spot for my duffel bag and other goods. This area was always comfortably warm regardless of the weather. Because of my position in Special Services, I could rest during the day and used the bunk but little, usually only for a while after visiting the left-over chow table at midnight.

The next few pages are a copy of my final souvenir edition of *"The Devil's Tale."* Enjoy!

The Devil's Tale – Souvenir Edition

Page 1

SOUVENIR EDITION   THE DEVIL'S TALE   VOLUME XII
****

Published daily in the Transport
Services Office

VOLUME XII, SOUVENIR EDITON

EDITOR................Norman Hansen

Asst. Editor..........Edward Delaney

Sports Editor.........James Roberts
Art Editor............Pat McLaughlin
Feature Writer........John Fizmaurice
Production Manager.....Richard Dixon

Transport Services Officer
         Lt. Paul Corwin

****

FROM THE TRANSPORT SERVICES OFFICER:

To all passengers:
     My sincere thanks to the men who
have so willingly devoted their time to
the ship's newspaper, movies, library,
public address system and entertainment.
     I also wish to express my appreci-
ation to all for the splendid manner in
which they have received our Transport
Services Program.
         Lt. Paul Corwin
         Transport Services Officer

****

FROM THE COMMANDING OFFICER OF TROOPS:

     The co-operation received by myself
and capable staff from all the troops a-
board is appreciated a great deal. I
wish to thank each and all for the effort
they have made for the benefit of the
rest.
     May all of you have the best of luck
and good fortune with your new tasks in
Japan. I am sure you will all be a true
representation of the American people as
a whole.
         James J. Stovall
         Lt. Col. Infantry

A WORD FROM THE CHAPLAIN

     "Be sure your sins will find you out.
Be not deceived; God is not mocked, for
whatsoever a man soweth, that shall also
shall he reap. The way of transgressors
is hard. For God shall bring every work
into judgement, with every secret thing,
whether it be good, or whether it be evil.
There is no pence, saith my God, to the
wicked. The soul that sinneth, it shall
die. His own iniquities shall take the
wicked himself, and he shall be bound with
the cords of his sins." From the Bible:
"What if I gain the thing I seek? A dream
a breath, a froth of fleeting joy--Who buys
a minute's mirth to wail a week, or seals
eternity to gain a toy?" Remember, somewhere a woman, mother, sweetheart, wife,
waits for your return, has faith in you,
prays for you. No other shares your
place in her heart. Soil not her faith
in you by sin. Keep for her sake a stain-
less name. Bring back to her a manhood
free from shame. God bless you.

****
FROM THE TRANSPORT COMMANDER

     It is my desire to extend heartiest
thanks and appreciation to Lt. Col. James
Stovall, and Officers and enlisted men,
for the exemplery manner in which all as-
signments were accomplished.
     I also wish to say that it has been an
honor having Col. and Mrs. Vinson aboard.
         Capt. Joseph F. Reynolds
         Transport Commander.

Page 2

```
*********************************************************************
SOUVENIR EDITION              THE DEVIL'S TALE              VOLUME XII
*********************************************************************
```

****

In this our final issue, we intro-
duce the fine upstanding lads who slaved
(that's a joke, son) day and night to
make possible a few pages of entertainment for the boys. When I say we enjoyed putting out the "Tale", I know I speak
for the entire staff. We have been just
one big "happy family" united to with-
stand the trials and tribulations that
invariably present themselves.

The staff as a whole and indivi-
ually wish to thank the "father", Lt.
Paul Corwin. His articles, his cooperation and his supervision have been
nothing short of excellent.

What is this mad-house? Is it a ward
in an insane asylum? Is it a Congress-
mans office? Is it a convention of Mongol
goat herds? No, none of these. It's the
Transport Services Office and the fever-
ish activity is toward the genral purpose of putting out a paper.

**************************************   **************************************

EDITOR-IN-CHIEF   NORMAN HANSEN   ASSISTANT EDITOR   EDWARD DELANEY

Norman attend-
ed the Univer-
sity of Wash-
ington where
he completed
one semester.
He had intend-
ed to major
in journaliism;
but as so freq-
quently happ-
ens, he got
that fateful
letter, and on
April 19, 1946
he was in. He took basic training at Ft.
McClellan in the infantry, and then came
to the ORD, where his only claim to
fame was being AWOL 6 nights out of 7.
(The seventh, he got a pass.) Oh yes,
he re-enlisted in May for 18 months.

Norm spends most of his time emul-
ating his favorite character, the invis-
ible man. He lives in Seattle, Wash.

Eddie spent his
time as a happy
civilian delfing
into the myster-
ies of Civil
Engineering at
Manhattan Coll-
ege in the Bronx
in New York.
Uncle Sam re-
quested his pre-
sence in April
of 46, and after
completing basic
at Fort McClel-
lan, came to the ORD and thence to us.
His "rapid-fire" shorthand proved inval-
uable in getting news from the short
wave. He was stencil cutter "par excell-
ence" except for a few nervous breakdowns
over the Chaplain's column. His home is
Waltham, Massachussetts.

Page 3

****

SOUVENIR EDITION   THE DEVIL'S TALE   VOLUME XII

****

WHO THE DEVIL? (Cont'd from preceeding page)

PAT McLAUGHLIN   STAFF CARTOONIST

Pat had just finished high school and was attempting to go to college, when the long arm of the draft board nailed him in March of 1946. He took basic at Aberdeen Proving Grounds, in the Ordnance, and then took Tech training at Edgewod Arsenal in the Chemical Warfare Service. During this training, he also put in a stint in the S-3 office. Pat is the world's greatest horizontal artist. He hails from Chicago Illinois.

****

JOHN FITZMAURICE   FEATURE WRITER

(Forward-Since I wrote the sketches of everyone else, anything outside of essential facts is no doubt grossly exagerated.) Just walk into Special Services Ofice, fan away the smoke, and, that bedragled figure you see hanging off the end of a Chesterfield, is "Fitz", or as he was christened, John Fitzmaurice. Fitz, after graduating from Grover Cleveland High Schol in Queens, N.Y., worked as a stock clerk in the home town, before answering "the cal" in September 1945. Fitz served in the capacity of ocupational counselor at Ft. Dix, N.J. until April of this year. Pfc Fitz tok his basic training at Camp Polk, Louisiana.

RICHARD DIXON   PRODUCTION MANAGER

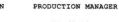

"Red" Dixon attended Bloomfield College where he was preparing to be an architectural engineer. He fooled the draft board by enlisting the day before he received his greetings. He took his basic in the signal corp at Camp Crowder, and Camp Polk, La. Red, the "man mountain Dean of the mimeograph machine", nightly coaxes, begs, pleads, threatens, cajoles, and gets gray hair over our mimeograph machine, which has been known to work for a whole 15 minutes straight-once. Red hails from Bloomfield, Iowa.

****

JAMES ROBERTS   SPORTS EDITOR

Jim completed high school and fearing the draft board's call, he put off college, and went to work as a station clerk in a railroad depot. He too got his fateful greetings and took infantry basic at Ft. McCllean. He then proceeded to the "DEVIL" by way of the ORD. His knowledge of sports helps to make those short wave reports interesting and understandable. Unfortunately, Jim is such a good "Joe" we can't think of any insults, so we'll end by mentioning his home town, Libby, Montana.

****

Page 4

```
******************************************************************************
SOUVENIR EDITION              THE DEVIL'S TALE              VOLUME XII
******************************************************************************
```

SHIP'S HISTORY

Back in 1943, someone got the bright idea that the Army needed a new Sherman tank carrier. Therefore, soon afterwards, in typical smooth Army efficiency, work was begun on the USS Marine Devil, a tank carrier. Also, in typically efficient Army style, the work was stopped half-way through production and the ship was converted into a troop carrier, which it is supposed to be now, in case anyone is interested.

The Devil was commissioned in Philadelphia in September of 1944 and for the rest of that year and until September of 1945 she ran replacements to the ETO, putting in, generally, to LeHavre.

In September, 1945 the Devil got its first glimpse of the Pacific when it went to Calcutta to bring back troops from the CBI to the states. The voyage was made via Saipan and Manila.

The Devil made two trips home from Korea, and that brings the total of men carried up to 55,000.

On the first trip to Korea, two men were washed overboard in a Pacific storm, and the ship was so shaken up, it had to put up in Honolulu for a rest, and to prevent a nervous breakdown, or some such thing.

On that ill-fated voyage, epidemics of measles broke out on the way to Frisco, and caused the Devil to be quarantined for 5 days in the harbor.

If anyone were to try to put bowling alleys on the Devil, (and you can't tell when someone might try) he would find that lengthwise he could get 10, and one across the beam. The Devil weighs a good 14,500 tons, and carries 2500 troops.

Whether the Devil is going to continue her weary journeys o'er the seas, stopping at exotic ports, and sailing on foreign oceans, we don't know. So far as we're concerned, after the Devil gets us where we're going, it can go where all good devils go.

That's right, you guessed it!

```
*******************************************
```

THE NEWS IN SPORTS

At the end of the 19th week of baseball in the major leagues, the Boston Red Sox appeared to have clinched the American League pennant, as they hold a 14 game lead over the New York Yankees. The Yanks and Detroit are still battling it out for 2nd place with the Yanks holding a 3 game edge. Here are the standings in the American League:

Team	Won	Lost	Per.
Boston	87	38	.696
New York	72	51	.585
Detroit	67	52	.563
Washington	61	62	.496
Cleveland	57	67	.460
Chicago	56	68	.452
St Louis	51	70	.421
Philadelphia	40	83	.325

In the National League, Brooklyn and St Louis are still maintaining their first place tie, each having a .617 percentage. The Chicago Cubs, have virtually lost all chances of repeating their 1945 performance as world champions, as they're now 9 full games off the pace. Boston appears to have a cinch on fourth as they lead the Cincinati Reds by 7 games. Following is a table of National League Standings:

Team	Won	Lost	Per.
Brooklyn	74	46	.617
St Louis	74	46	.617
Chicago	64	54	.542
Boston	59	57	.509
Cincinatti	54	66	.450
New York	52	66	.441
Philadelphia	49	69	.415
Pittsburg	46	68	.404

The leading hitter in the American League is Mickey Vernon of Washington, who is batting .344 to hold a 4 point lead over Ted Williams of the Boston Red Sox. Behind Williams are Pesky of Boston with .338, and a tie between Appling of Chicago and Dom DiMaggio of Boston who each have a .328 percentage.

(Cont'd on page 6 Col 2)

Page 5

****
SOUVENIR EDITION   THE DEVIL'S TALE   VOLUME XII
****

DEAR DIARY

SATURDAY

Left Seattle today at 4:30. We bid a fond adieu to the dear old ORD to a new home aboard the Devil (unsuspecting fools that we were). The first night was calm and everyone was exploring our new surroundings and looking at the Washington coastline.

SUNDAY

Sunday dawned bright and clear, and early risers got their last look at good old terra firma. There were movies on deck and all were looking forward to a pleasant journey.

MONDAY

Disillusionment! Our first look at old Pop Neptune when he was kicking his heels up. The first ravages of mal-do-mer swept the ship and No. 1 issue of the Devil came out.

TUESDAY

ULP! Another day like the previous one--foggy, rainy, and rough. To top it all off, we had an abandon ship drill and all hands rushed topside, life-jackets and all. There were several wet "Joes" that night. We also escaped hitting a pair of floating mines.

WEDNESDAY

Fog again. It must be this Aleutian climate. The sea, however, calmed down, and most of us were recuperating slowly. Today, in the Inferno (galley) we got the first of a series of Spam sandwich lunches.

THURSDAY

That old demon Fog hovered all around us again today. It lifted a little in the afternoon, and someone started the rumor that the sun had come through for a minute.
****

FRIDAY

Today at 12:23, we passed the dateline and lost Saturday. We are finally getting out of the clutches of the Aleutian fog. The weather promises to be much better for the rest of the trip.

SUNDAY

Ah, sunshine!! Today was one of the best days so far. Blue skies, blue sea, ah, for the life of a sailor. The Yugoslav situation had gotten down to a lot of charges and counter charges. The Red Sox had the American League pennant clinched with a 14 game lead. St Louis and Brooklyn were battling it out for first place in the National League.

MONDAY

Another good day. We are heading south and the holds have gotten hot and sticky. I suppose we'll have it real hot before we get to Japan. All sea-sickness was forgotten and everyone was counting the days to go.

TUESDAY

Real dirty weather today. The ground swells were running high and the old seasickness was returning to a few unfortunates. Movies were called off on the deck tonight because of the weather.

WEDNESDAY

We managed to skirt the end of a typhoon last night and had another debarkation drill today. The sea, however, continued rough and we in Special Services spent our time chasing chairs, typewriters and our cantankerous Mimeograph machine across the floor.
****

THE SHIP'S LOG

Here's our position as of 28 August 1946:
    Latitude 39° 43' N
    Longitude 116° 25' E
    Distance last 24 hours--375 miles
    Total distance from Seattle--3791 Miles
    Average speed--15.7 knots

Page 6

```
*******************************************************************************
SOUVENIR EDITION              THE DEVIL'S TALE                    VOLUME XII
*******************************************************************************
```

WHAT A MESS ! ! !

While most of you fair voyageurs sat (or stood) complacently munching your victuals during the Devil's trip to the Orient, you probably had no idea that you all together consumed enough food to keep a herd of good sized elephants healthy and happy for a good long time. That is, if the elephants didn't mind sandwiches and coffee for lunch every day.

On the whole, our food was exceptionally good, considering it was obtained on the middle of the Pacific Ocean and prepared in surroundings that don't exactly rival the Waldorf-Astoria's.

Here's a typical list of foodstuffs consumed on a Sunday:

```
600 lbs. sausage or
125 lbs meat and eggs
420 dozen eggs
4800 slices bread
72 lbs jam
120 lbs butter
216 pts evaporated milk
21 cases grapefruit
100 lbs cooked cereal
2400 units dry cereal
250 lbs sugar
160 lbs coffee
2700 lbs chicken
120 gals green peas
900 lbs potatoes
34 gals pickles
2400 cups ice cream
```

As you can see, that's quite a hunk of food in any man's language. All in all the food consumed on the entire trip reads something like this:

```
8400 lbs sausage
100,00 slices bread
1680 lbs butter
4200 lbs cookies
4580 lbs coffee
```

```
**************************************
```

A WORD OF THANKS

This is a little tribute to Sgt. John Moore, and Pvt. Irving Magilnik, Projectionists "extraordinaire" as well as their assistants Pfc. Raphael and Pfc. Shea for their fine work in bringing movies to the men on board each night, despite the trials and tribulations usually associated with a projector. Thanks - job well done.

THE NEWS IN PORTS
(Cont'd from page 5 col 2)

Williams is leading the league in home runs with 33, followed by Hank Greenberg of Detroit who has clouted 26 round trippers. George Case, speed outfielder from Cleveland, has stolen 27 bases to lead the league in that department, and Boo Ferriss of Boston is the league's leading pitcher, having won 23 and lost only 4.

In the senior circuit, Stan Musial of St. Louis is batting .380, to hold a 15 point margin over John Hopp of Boston. Hopp, batting .365 is followed by Dixie Walker of Brooklyn, with .350, Mize of New York 339, Gordon of New York .309, and Phil Cavaretta of Chicago with .306.

Mize has socked 22 homeruns to lead the league, and Pete Reiser of Brooklyn is the leading base-stealer with 27. Howie Pollet of St. Louis has shown himself to be a big factor in the Cards pennant drive, as he has won 16 games to take top pitching honors.

It is expected that the pennant race in the National League will be a battle between Brooklyn and St Louis right down to the final game, with the winner meeting the Boston Red Sox in the World Series in October.

The World Series this year is going to be held on a pre-war basis. At a meeting held in Chicago, recently, with Commissioner Happy Chandler presiding, it was decided to return the pre-war practice of shifting the scenes of the games 3 times. During the war, the first 3 games were held in one city, and the last 4, if necessary, in the other city.

This year, however, the first 2 games will be played in the National League Park the next 3 in the American League Park, and the last 2 if necessary back at the original site.

Presidents Ford Frick of the National League and William Harridge of the American League were present at the meeting along with representatives from each of the first 3 teams in both leagues, which included Boston, New York, and Detroit in the American League, and Brooklyn, St Louis, and Chicago in the National League.

Page 7

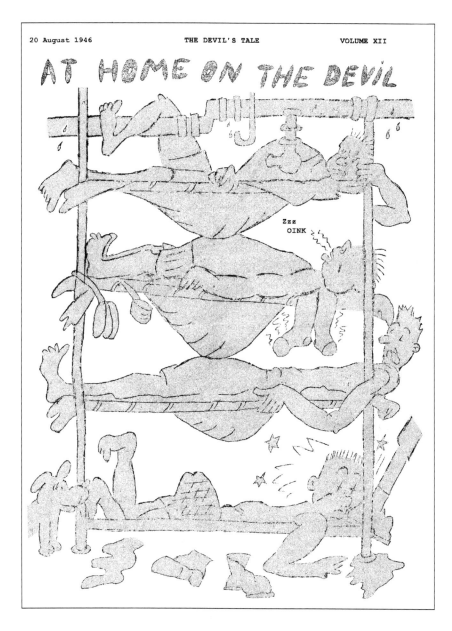

Page 8

Typhoon

The worst weather we experienced was the outer edge of a typhoon off the Aleutian Islands. Virtually everyone got seasick and there was vomit nearly everywhere. I was pleased that keeping busy, eating regularly and breathing lots of fresh air saved me from that. But, oh! The odor! In my mind, I can smell it still.

The ship swayed dramatically from side to side in slow, lazy rolls. It tipped so far that some portholes had to be buckled tight. For many of the troops, it was quite frightening, but officers on the bridge assured me that, although this was about the most rolling they had experienced, we were a long way from being in danger. Also, unlike the *Titanic*, the *USS Marine Devil* encountered no ice bergs. The seagulls trailing the ship seemed to enjoy it. Could that be because so many food scraps were thrown overboard and some of it was conveniently partially digested?

I Will if You Will

A friend aboard this ship was Don Robinson from Wenatchee, Washington. We often played chess on the cruise to Japan. Don and I were interrupted in our chess game by a sergeant who circulated around the ship trying to sell troopers on the notion of becoming a paratrooper. He made it sound exciting, challenging and remunerative (fifty dollars per month jump pay).

While Don was whupping me again at the chess board, we talked about the paratrooper proposition. The money was enticing. After five qualifying parachute jumps, we had to make just one jump every three months to remain qualified and collect jump pay. The challenge and the glory of being something special appealed to us. Hey, the girls go for that! Anyway, we each said, "I will if you will." Thus, we became part of the six-hundred-plus people who volunteered for jump school—all of us knowing that we could drop out at any time. Thus began an experience I cherish to this day. Successfully completing Jump School was a tremendous boost to my self-confidence that worked in my favor for the rest of my life. *Carpe diem!*

Entering Yokohama Bay

As our ship, the *USS Marine Devil*, came into Yokohama Bay early in the afternoon and anchored offshore, I was struck by the powerful odor from the bay and thought to myself, "So, this is how the Orient smells." My nose could detect rice, spices and camphor. The aromas were misleading, because at this time the waters of the Bay were simply filthy.

Standing by the rail, I leaned over to look at something moving in the water. For high school graduation, my parents had bought me an expensive Parker fountain pen that I treasured. Of course, at this moment, it slipped out of my shirt pocket and fell *kerplunk!* into the water. I nearly cried as I watched my new pen slowly disappear beneath the murky waters.

Soon, small Japanese boats hovered around the ship. Some of them had souvenirs to sell. Others came to beg food, for Japan's economy was still having problems. I became aware of my own good fortune when I observed a young Japanese man scoop up an orange rind tossed over the railing and greedily suck at the remnants of orange stuck to the peels. Welcome to Japan!

It had been somewhat over a year since General MacArthur became Supreme Commander of the Allied Forces and, though he'd worked wonders, there was room for improvement.

Map of Japan

Paratrooper Jump School

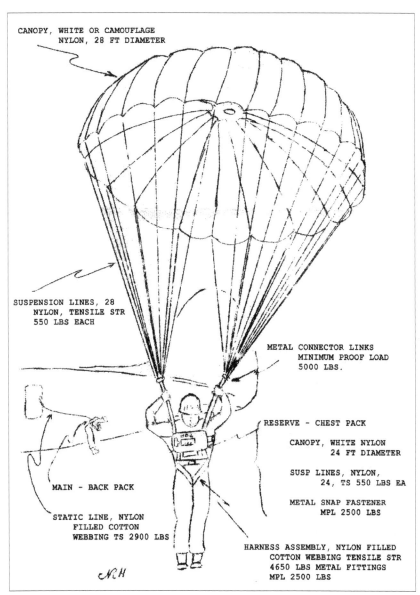

CANOPY, WHITE OR CAMOUFLAGE
NYLON, 28 FT DIAMETER

SUSPENSION LINES, 28
NYLON, TENSILE STR
550 LBS EACH

METAL CONNECTOR LINKS
MINIMUM PROOF LOAD
5000 LBS.

RESERVE - CHEST PACK

CANOPY, WHITE NYLON
24 FT DIAMETER

SUSP LINES, NYLON,
24, TS 550 LBS EA

METAL SNAP FASTENER
MPL 2500 LBS

MAIN - BACK PACK

STATIC LINE, NYLON
FILLED COTTON
WEBBING TS 2900 LBS

HARNESS ASSEMBLY, NYLON FILLED
COTTON WEBBING TENSILE STR
4650 LBS METAL FITTINGS
MPL 2500 LBS

*Assembly Troop Type T-7 with Quick Release Box and Modified
Reserve, a figure reproduced from handouts I received in 1946.*

Paratrooper Training Begins

At the "Repple Depple" (Replacement Depot) in Yokohama, we were met by one of the most imposing physical specimens of humanity I have ever seen. Sergeant First Class Bator sported a 56-inch chest and a 26-inch waist. Extremely powerful and athletic, I was told that he had once been ranked 9th Lightweight Boxer in the World. He coached our boxing team and it went undefeated during my time in Japan.

Sergeant Bator challenged anyone to step forward and fight. Of course, no one was foolish enough to accept. Finally, he chose the largest volunteer and invited him to stand on his shoulders while he did push-ups. He made it look easy with over 250 pounds on his back and shoulders. I soon learned first-hand and in great detail that push-ups were a big thing in the paratroopers.

Sergeant Bator was one rung below master sergeant, and he readily admitted that he more than once had turned down a promotion to Master solely on the basis of his last name.

From the Repple Depple we went directly to barracks in Camp Schimmelpfennig in Sendai. After a day or so of settling in, orientation, more shots, fatigue, etc., we were sent by a narrow-gauge train, nicknamed the "Toonerville Trolley," the twenty-five miles up to Carelus Field in Yamoto where jump training started.

Jump Preparation

One of the most exciting and memorable aspects of my stay in Japan was the three weeks of training for parachute jumping. (Why do they call it "jumping" when it's more like falling?)

The six hundred men who had volunteered for parachute training were separated out upon arrival in Japan, and we soon went to Carelus Field Operations at the Yamoto base.

March 1947 – C-46 Curtis Commando refueling on the apron in front of the hangar at Carelus Field at Yamoto

March 1947 — Airplane hangar at Carelus Field Operations
in Yamoto, Japan

This training was rigorous and "no nonsense" from the beginning. We lived in Quonset huts and were expected to be ready for the day's program by 0500 hours: clean, shaved and in pressed fatigues. (How the hell?) Each morning, the sergeants stood in the men's room and watched to be certain each soldier had actually shaved. If you didn't pass inspection, you were sent back to rectify the problem.

I was nineteen years of age, fair-skinned with light blond hair, and my beard had barely begun to show. So, every day, I faithfully lathered up and scraped away the soap with a razor sans blade and actually inserted a blade only about every three days or so to shave properly.

March 1947 — Carelus Field Operations in Yamoto with scaffolding, broken windows and missing siding while underging renovation. The aircraft hangar is in the background on the left. The rightmost sign includes "Elevation 7 Feet" while the leftmost sign reads "11ᵗʰ Troop Carrier Division Operations, Power Section"

A Quonset hut being placed at the 598th Engineer Base in Japan
Image by US Army Corps of Engineers

Quonset huts were corrugated portable metal buildings; they were used all over the Pacific in WWII. They had straight, flat ends and a rounded roof and were long enough to hold fifteen canvas cots down each side of a spacious aisle. By placing your fatigues neatly folded on the canvas cot, covering them with a blanket and sleeping on them, you could actually achieve the effect of pressing them.

Our Quonset hut was situated next to a large ditch filled with stagnant water that was ideal for breeding mosquitoes. One morning, I counted twenty-six bites on my arms and face, the only places on my body not under cover. Although we were very tired by bedtime, going to sleep was difficult with all the buzzing, slapping and swearing.

At the end of the training program, we were issued a certificate testifying to a successful completion and we were awarded silver paratrooper wings, which we wore with pride.

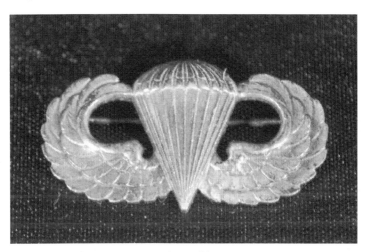

Paratrooper wings earned by Norman Hansen

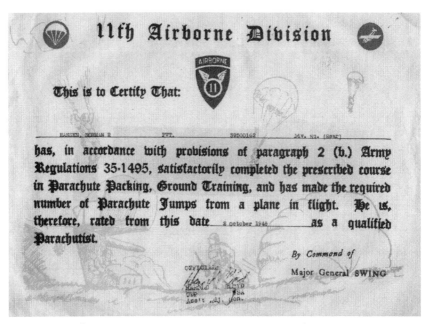

October 2ⁿᵈ, 1946 — Paratrooper certification, 11ᵗʰ Airborne Division

Latino on the Practice Tower

1946 — Paratrooper training jump tower similar to the ones we used

Parachute jumping was strictly on a volunteer basis. From the more than 600 original volunteers, slightly less than 300 soldiers qualified. The remaining troops were injured or unable to meet the demands of training.

For training purposes, there was a twenty- to thirty-foot high tower. On the top was a 2-foot by 4-foot framework resembling the door of a plane. A parachute harness was hitched to a snap fastener and then to a pulley on a cable, where a group was waiting to pull the harness back for the next trainee. You would jump out and slide *way* down along the cable into a sawdust bin. This was to teach the proper form for exiting a plane sideways in a crouch and the right way to land. This came to be a lot of fun. Is this where modern recreational zip lines got started?

For the very first guy in our platoon that went up on this tower, the sergeant forgot to hook the snap ring to the cable. There were huge boulders below at the base. He plummeted down toward them, landed between two of them and rolled over. We all rushed to the side and looked down over the edge. There were ten of us in our stick on that big platform. I heard someone say, "Oh my god!" The jumper was a Latino kid, who stood up, shook himself and said "*I kweet, somebody geet hurt doin thees!*"

I can't say that I blame him. It's lucky he survived. It's hard to believe that he wasn't even injured. He must have been a natural for that business.

The Paratroop Shuffle

We trained in platoons of ten men each. The particular platoon I was assigned to happened to contain three commissioned officers, a captain and two lieutenants. One morning, our regular sergeant was ill and we got a substitute, a newly-arrived sergeant from Fort Benning.

All went well until somewhere down the road the sergeant took the platoon for a "run" along the rice paddies. A paratroop "run" was really just jogging, hence we called it the "Paratroop Shuffle." The sergeant was not in good shape, and after about an hour we commenced to kid him about it. "Come on Sarge, let's speed it up a bit!" and "Is this how they do it in Fort Benning?"

Picture of rice fields, taken from the train to (or from) Yamoto. The straight, white lines are raised walkways separating each field where our platoon was jogging. Rice plants are growing in about six inches of water. In the distant background is Carelus Field.

Finally, he gasped and said, "Okay, maybe I'm out of shape, but I can do push-ups. Men, hit the lean and rest [push-up position] and we'll do push-ups!" We did push-ups until *he* could finally do no more.

After more teasing, he lost his temper and proceeded to swear at us. Then he took us back to Carelus Field on the concrete apron in front of the hangars. We were in a line and he told us to jog until someone dropped out. Then he stood in the middle of what would become a large square, and at each corner came the command, "Column right!"

March 1947 – We jogged for hours around this concrete apron at Carelus Field

This went on for nearly two hours, until a messenger came trotting out and told him that we needed to move along. "Platoon, Halt!" came his command.

He thereupon apologized profusely for his intemperate language and said that we would all make good paratroopers. The man leading our patrol this whole time, a captain not wearing any insignia, stepped forward and said, "Sergeant, I am Captain So-and-so, and I am glad to hear you apologize."

The sergeant's jaw dropped when he realized how close he had come to serious trouble with his career. The rest of us were proud of ourselves for enduring and not quitting. It strongly reinforced the notion that paratroopers were tough.

A Quiet Glide

As part of our parachute training, we were given a ride in a glider— probably a Waco CG-4A, which can carry twelve troopers. The basic idea of using gliders in the Army Air Mobile was just beginning to be explored. The thinking was that inexpensive gliders, holding ten or so troops with gear, could be towed to arrive and land in a spot behind enemy lines. The troops would harass the enemy supply lines, causing the enemy to deploy their troops well in excess of our glider-load.

For the experience, our platoon of ten men was loaded into a glider. A long, strong tow line led to a small plane which towed us up and out high over the ocean, whereupon our glider pilot cut us loose. For about ten minutes, he flew lazy circles in the air and then headed for the LZ (landing zone).

Example of Waco CG-4A Glider
Image courtesy of Budd Davisson

My recollection of the experience was one of peace and quiet. It seemed to affect my mates the same way, for we hesitated to break the reverie by speaking. Just that single glider ride qualified us to wear, along with the paratrooper's emblem, glider wings. Unfortunately, it did not bring extra pay.

As a sidebar to the glider experience, the guys in the office, always looking for some entertainment, came upon a glider blown upside down by a windstorm. They took a photo of one of us crawling out of it, as if in an accident. It was good for a laugh. I dearly wish I had a copy of that picture.

Glider wings earned by Norman Hansen

Paratrooper Qualifying

*June 1947 — Watching parachute training outside of our office
building, looking east across the rice paddies to a grassy field used as
a drop zone. The white strip beyond the fence is the take-off and
landing strip for Piper Cubs.*

The drop zone was about a mile or so away from our offices, beyond the fence that separated our office building from a small landing strip.

With a parachute twenty-eight feet across in ordinary atmospheric conditions, you fall about sixteen feet per second. This results in a pretty hard landing. I forget exactly, but it's something like jumping off a ten-foot building.

Out of the seven jumps I made, I managed to land and remain upright on only two of the jumps. I think the ten inches of snow on the DZ (drop zone) helped on those two successful landings. I fell down on the other five jumps.

We practiced five points of contact when landing: the balls of your feet came first, then the next four points as you fell and rolled. In spite of the opening on top of the chute, it was very difficult to control oscillation. So, I determined my own five points of contact... my heels, my butt three times and the back of my head! Ouch!

Expert parachutists claim that a standing landing is easy. They say to pull all your risers down and, just before contact, let them loose and they will "pop" the chute to a temporary stop, leaving a short drop to earth. I never had the opportunity to try this because of oscillations causing my chute to swing rather briskly.

Qualifying Jumps

Say what you will, but parachute jumping was scary. Rolf Mogster, my nephew, tells me that he can't figure why anyone would jump out of a perfectly good airplane. Our equipment was less efficient than the parachutes they are using now. Our Type T-7 parachutes had a twenty-eight-foot diameter canopy with a hole in the middle. They were round; these were neither the winged type nor the sport parachutes we have today. The T-7 has faster descent speed and excessive oscillations; they were more dangerous than today's equipment. However, there is something good to be said for speed of descent if you're under fire.

One of the first things they did was take us to watch the parachute packers in the packing shed. There they had laid out a parachute, over ninety feet in length, on a long, narrow table designed for this job.

The sergeant said, "They pack these very carefully, but here's what you *can* do." He gathered up the nylon canopy and risers, jammed them into the pack, put the top over and sewed it back down the way it belonged. Then he strapped the pack on, went up in a little airplane and made a successful jump with that hastily packed parachute. The sergeant's intent was to show us that packing a parachute was pretty safe and foolproof. And it was.

As we were both training and staying at Carelus Field, our qualifying jumps started from there. On a brisk Monday morning, I—along with twenty-nine rather frightened others—was harnessed up into parachute gear and loaded into a C-46 Curtis Commando. We were organized into "sticks" of ten. Ours would be the first stick to jump.

March 1946 — Curtis Commando C-46, a high altitude, long range transport plane with a single door on the port side.
It could carry 30 troopers.

We were making our first pass at 1,200 feet and a speed of about 120 miles per hour over the drop zone in Sendai when our jumpmaster commanded, "Stand up and hook up. Each trooper, check the harness and hook-up of the man in front of you. Now, close up to the man in front." With the stick in position, the front man crouched by the open door where the wind was whipping past. The jumpmaster waited until the plane was in position and then touched the back of number one's leg. Off we went! Before we knew it, the parachutes had popped open and we were floating (rather rapidly!) down toward the grassy field. By the time we had checked our canopy and looked for the horizon, we had crashed safely to the ground. The trip down took about twenty seconds. Gathering up our nylon chutes, we shared a great feeling of exhilaration, mixed with the knowledge that we had to do it all over again this same day.

So, back we went on the "Toonerville Trolley" for our second qualifying jump. We could fit two qualifying jumps in one day, so it took us three days to finish all five. Along with a great sense of accomplishment was the awful feeling one held for those few who could not force themselves to make another jump.

March 1946 — Trainees on the "Toonerville Trolley" returning from a jump. One of these soldiers looks worried.

On the first jump, we didn't know what to expect and were not very frightened. For the second jump, we were sort of numb and just going through the motions. At the third jump on the second day, it was purely frightening, and after a night's broken sleep we were not sure we could go through with it. But, after landing that one, we began to see the joy of it and looked forward to more. However, during the rest of my life, I never did parachute from an airplane again.

Clancy and I had a twenty-five dollar bet on who would make the first civilian jump after our time in the army. Nobody collected, although I once seriously considered being a "smoke jumper" and fighting summer forest fires.

March 1946 — Trainees on the train back from a jump,
the first of two jumps that day.

Catching a Double Cigarette Roll

I saw an amazing thing when we did our qualifying jumps. The DZ was a busy place during training sessions. There were thirty people in each of three C-46 airplanes. A stick of ten would jump out on each pass. You would stand up and hook the strap on the back of your chute over the cable. When you got out the door, you were close together, one after another. After falling ninety feet, the static line pulled the pack off the back of the chute, broke away and the chute popped open. This created quite a shock on your harness and you learned to wear it uncomfortably tight.

They told us that once in ten thousand times, you'd have a streamer or "cigarette roll" due to static electricity, moisture or something else. If this happens, the chute won't open; it will twist around, and the air will go through the top of it without opening the canopy. In the rare case your main chute doesn't work, you have a reserve chute strapped on your front. It has a D-ring and you reach down and pull to open it. Unlike the twenty-eight-foot-wide main chute, this reserve chute was only twenty-four feet in diameter, but it would save your buns.

We were told that when you come out of the plane, one of the first things you do when the chute opens is to grab the risers, pull them apart and look up to make sure it's completely inflated. You need to be sure that you don't have a riser strapped over the top of the canopy. If you do have a "Mae West" or "Dolly Parton" then you need to pull that riser off of there.

During our training, there were three airplanes, each dropping a stick of ten during each pass, so there could be three or four layers of men in the air at one time.

In one instance, I was pretty well along on my jump and it was going as planned, but I looked up to check my chute anyway. In a group above me, a guy had a streamer! He pulled his reserve chute right away, and he had *another* streamer! Some other guy between us in another stick saw him coming and pulled his chute over toward him. As the first guy came hurtling by, this man stuck his boot out and snagged it under the edge of the nylon, wrapped his arms around the streamer and pulled it in! He hung on tightly to that chute, and they both rode the same chute down. What a sight to see!

Later, they held a parade in our camp to honor this hero.

Can you imagine being alert enough, at that speed and in the midst of all that activity, to intercept him and hang on? Oh, that poor guy falling—he must have been petrified. I understand that he never went back up, and that was it. You can quit anytime, and I think he did. In fact, we started with over 600 volunteers and only 295 qualified. Some events evoke strong emotions and etch themselves in your mind. This is one event I never forgot.

Static Line Problems

Each parachute has a strap called a "static line" hooked onto the back of the pack with a breakable cord that pulls out your chute. It has a tensile strength of less than a hundred pounds. It breaks off the back of the pack after it pulls out the parachute. They told us many, many times how to use the static line: This cord comes around here and around there, you grab it there, and you snap it onto the static line. You throw it on down the line when you come up to the door to make room for the next man, and then jump.

On one jump, JD Owen, a good old Southern boy and one of my best friends in camp, was directly in front of me in the line. JD wrapped the static line the *wrong* way around his arm and created a big problem. When he jumped and hit the end of the line, it caught him and twisted him, and he was slowed up and hanging on it from the airplane. I followed him out the door and almost hit him! When JD got down to the ground, his fatigue jacket was torn from his wrist all the way down to the bottom seam, and his entire arm was badly bruised. You see, you don't just drop: The plane is leaving you much faster than you're dropping. It's traveling some 120 miles per hour and you can't achieve that speed in the 90 feet or so that you have.

Another good friend, LeRoy Edel, somehow clipped his static line snap-ring *onto* the cable on his second qualifying jump, rather than *over* it. If it had slipped off the cable, it would not have pulled out his main chute. He was very lucky that it held long enough to pull his chute open *before* it slipped off the cable. We became aware of it only after, on the ground, we discovered that the entire static line and snap fastener were still attached to his parachute! He said he almost fainted when he saw the line and fastener still there.

It Takes More Than Guts

Some events are so emotionally loaded that they stick in your mind and reawaken your original strong emotional feelings.

On our plane, one of the men taking parachute training was a WW II soldier who had been awarded the Distinguished Service Cross for bravery. That he was an unusually courageous man was a given.

He had made his first jump and was on the plane about to make his second jump. When it was time for his stick to leave the plane, he simply froze up. He could not make himself go out the door. Crying uncontrollably, he sat back down.

I think all the rest of us felt so badly for our hero that there wasn't a dry eye in the airplane. It must have hurt him terribly for the rest of his life. I know that I still feel badly for him.

Fort Benning Stories

There were a lot of stories that came out of Fort Benning, Georgia, where stateside troopers were trained. In talk sessions and in comparing notes among the paratroopers, we heard many stories, of which several remain with me to this day.

Backing Out

In Fort Benning, Georgia they jumped out of C-47s. In comparison, on our C-46s, we had but one door on the port side so we jumped out of just one side of the plane. But on C-47s, they have two doors and jump two sticks, one on each side. The story was that one fellow at the end of his stick froze up, crying "No! No!" and backed away from the door—and backed right out the other side. Well, it *could* have happened.

Monkey Business

They also told this story about a monkey at Fort Benning that loved to jump. He just loved parachute jumping. But they lost him one day. The monkey climbed hand-over-hand up the risers and collapsed the chute, and it killed him. I don't know how much to trust about the stories the paratroopers used to tell in bull sessions. They even claimed they had a German Shepherd that enjoyed parachuting.

Jeep Droppings

This story goes that they once took a Jeep up in the Lockheed Hercules C-130 and attached a parachute on each corner of the Jeep. Then, they pushed it out the back ramp while they were flying over the DZ. The parachutes opened up all right. But they didn't count on one thing: The chutes were so close to each other they robbed air from each other. One would collapse, and then it would open and prevent air from reaching another, until another chute popped open again, rocking back and forth wildly all the way down and falling a great deal faster than intended. Until *boom!* There was a bunch of rubble on the ground. Talk about Jeep droppings!

Office Life

November 1946 – Norman Hansen at the end of a day in the office, with Daisy and a Coke. The clock indicates 5:41 pm and I'm trying to study algebra for my correspondence course.

What did I do in Japan? I was a clerk typist in the G-4 (general staff office) in charge of supplies and equipment. I typed up TO&E (table of order and equipment), I typed any correspondence that the captain wanted and I answered the phone. I was his clerk. I was also in charge of the motor pool. That meant that I was responsible for checking out and checking in vehicles. This is rather like a library for cars. I was not responsible for maintenance. Maybe those duties don't seem like much, but they certainly kept me busy.

My boss, Captain C. C. Lumpkin, was a nice guy from Arkansas and was part Native American. He was a bright man and easy going. But... any letter he sent out under his name was required to be typed perfectly with no erasures. So, even though I had typing classes in high school and could do Touch Typing, I had to learn to slowly hunt-and-peck every letter to ensure perfection. It went very slowly. It was difficult or impossible to correct carbon copies with erasures that did not jump out at you. This might be why I remained a cautious hunt-and-peck typist the rest of my life.

August 1947 — Captain Lumpkin, my boss, standing outside Building C-102 in Sendai, Japan

In the photo of Captain Lumpkin, notice how he "bloused" his trousers on the top of his jump boots. This is a typical "show off" paratrooper tactic. Also, to be done correctly, the boots had to be laced up with white nylon from parachute risers.

TO&E

The "Table of Organization and Equipment" is a list of every item the company had—or should have had—including personnel. For instance, an entry might look somewhat like this:

Helmet, steel, insulated, No.14, 3axxx, qty. 4,000

Or

Captain, ---, qty. 34

The quantity of "captains" is not an inventory, but the number deemed to be necessary for the company.

Every item has its name, description, perhaps an Army number and the quantity the division was allotted. All this had to be recorded in complete and unambiguous detail. These lists were used for such things as reordering supplies, getting new personnel and filling spots with promotions. Every unit in the army had its own TO&E, and they were important.

One of my jobs was to use an IBM Selectric typewriter to make copies of the TO&E for the 11th Airborne Division Headquarters. These copies were on legal sized paper (8½ by 14 inches) and were to be done in triplicate, using carbon paper. Carbon paper seems so old-fashioned now, but it was very up to date and modern in 1946.

When I had to type a letter for Captain Lumpkin, it had to be accurate in every respect before he would accept it. He would accept erasures, but not on his personal correspondence. Many times, I would make a small error and have to start all over!

For copying the TO&E, I was allowed to make corrections. However, taking the papers out of the typewriter, erasing errors on each of the three copies and replacing it all accurately in the typewriter was a real pain and very time-consuming. Working on it in my "spare" time, it still took over a month to complete. There were times I would look for something else to do to avoid the dreaded monotony of this task.

When the TO&E was done, the three copies would barely fit in an apple box. This project literally destroyed my typing skill. Being much in fear of making a mistake, I reverted to the Columbus method of typing: find a key and land on it. Even to this day, several decades later, I need to look at the keyboard while typing.

If this task was all "make work," the result was gratifying when Captain Lumpkin said, "Now, Hansen, take all the TO&Es on the train to Headquarters in Sapporo, up north on Hokkaido Island."

Trip to Sapporo

I took the train to Sapporo to deliver my apple box full of the 11th Airborne Division's TO&E in the first week in January of 1947. I had typed these myself in triplicate, and the trip was, in part, a reward for my diligent work. On the journey north and on the way back, I snapped a number of good travel photos with my new Mercury II 35 mm camera.

January 1947 — Sendai Station narrow gauge rail for steam engines.
Note the large coal bin and steam shovel in distant right.

January 1947 — Boarding the train and getting ready to leave from Sendai Station

January 1947 — Seemingly endless mountains along the route during the return trip. The rice paddies in the foreground are fallow, awaiting spring planting. In preparation for this, the plants are seeded very close together to make bundles of rice plants, which are then spaced out across the paddies at the appropriate time.

January 1947 — Winter scene en route

January 1947 — We paused at Noheji Station on the way to Chibiki Station. Note the water tower for our steam engines.

When the train reached Aomori, a town on the northern tip of Honshu, it was unhooked and loaded car by car, with passengers still on them, onto a large ferry boat. While this was happening, I looked out the window and saw a man carrying a limp form, an obviously drowned boy from the water of the ocean beach. I had been indoctrinated to believe that the Japanese people were stoic, but the look of pure anguish on that man's face is permanently etched in my memory. There is no doubt in my mind that the Japanese people love their children very much.

*January 1947 — Train station with a connection to load
railroad cars onto the ferry boat.*

Like our ferry system in Washington State, ferry passengers in
Aomori were allowed on deck. It was a five-hour ferry boat ride to
Hakodati, followed by a train ride to Sapporo. On deck, I was
approached by three officers and two sergeants. I was only a private
first class. One of them said, "Soldier, do you play pinochle?"

"Yes, Sir, a little bit," I replied. Pinochle was an entertainment mainstay in my house for many years, and I was actually a fairly experienced player.

"Good." I played double-deck pinochle with them for nearly five hours. It was fun, entertaining and educational besides helping pass the time for nearly five hours.

I truly wish I had a clearer memory of Sapporo, but time (nearly seventy years) has eroded most of the details. On the far north island of Hokkaido, the city of Sapporo was in the throes of winter. I recall massive snowdrifts in town of nearly twenty feet in height and tunnels through them to places of business.

Winter in Sapporo is a serious matter. The 1940 Winter Olympics were to have been held in Sapporo, but the games were canceled by the onset of World War II. Much later, Sapporo hosted the 1972 Winter Olympics.

Never Volunteer

I was told, more than once, that in the army, one should never volunteer. I did, and... well, read this and you can make up your mind.

As clerical workers, we had Saturday afternoons free. However, on a rotating basis, one NCO (non-commissioned officer) was designated C.Q., "charge of quarters" (clerk of the day), which meant they had to stay and be available for anything that needed attention. All the officers were gone. There had to be somebody there to answer the phone in case of emergencies. Since I had nothing else pressing, I rashly volunteered to cover for Corporal Edel, who claimed some lame excuse for why he couldn't do the duty.

All was well until about 2 p.m. when the phone rang. "Eleventh Airborne, Rear Echelon, Corporal Hansen, Sir," I answered.

A Lieutenant Colonel from Headquarters in Sapporo, sounding somewhat distraught, said his wife was in labor and desperately needed to go to the hospital in Camp Schimmelpfennig. Could they fly her in their jet to the hospital?

"Yes, Sir. I will try!"

The problem was that the camp's hospital did not have its own airport. Although we had a small runway by our office building, it wasn't big enough for a jet to land. The closest runway that might handle a jet was in our drop zone was a couple of miles from the hospital. So, the proposal was to land the jet at the DZ, send a small L-14 to hop over the intervening rice paddies to meet the jet coming from Sapporo and bring the patient to the street in front of the hospital.

First, I had to determine if that jet could land and take off from the facilities at the Drop Zone. I called them, got the OK, and they arranged for an L-14. This small plane had a compartment in the fuselage where a person could lie down. It had a hinged panel the length of the patient's bed.

Piper L-14
Photo by David Álvarez López

An airplane similar to our Piper L-14 Army Cruiser
Stock photo from Dreamstime

Next, I contacted the hospital, where they assembled a medical team. Then I called the MPs (military police) to close the street in front of the hospital, far enough back that they could land the L-4 on the street. The road was designed for this purpose in case of medical emergencies—it had room to land these little Piper Cubs right in front of the building. I called back to the Lieutenant Colonel in Sapporo and, with everything set up, the flights all went well.

For me, it was a harrowing experience, but was very gratifying. You know, when you get in those situations, you do what needs to be done, even if you're just taking the office duty for a friend.

As far as I know, they did not name the baby after me.

Well, what do you think? Next time, should I follow the advice and play it safe, or take my risks?

The Longest Jump

Our office looked out over the drop zone. We had binoculars and a stop watch. We would measure how long it would take a stick from the time it opened to when it landed. The average was around twenty seconds. They jumped from about 1200 feet—not real high. In fact, that's considered low level jumping. When they trained in Fort Benning, Georgia, they flew even lower and made one jump from 250 feet, and that is quite dangerous.

As we were watching one day, the last trooper at the end of a stick kind of hovered when he got down part way. The next thing we knew, he'd caught an updraft and went up higher than the airplane! You can steer to some extent with the risers that come out just above your shoulders. You can grab them and pull an edge of a chute down, which causes it to slip in that direction. The trooper pulled himself out of that situation and began descending once more. Unfortunately, he got caught in the updraft *again*. He spent two and a half minutes parachuting from 1200 feet. What a ride. I can imagine him being both scared and exhilarated. I know I would have been.

Cargo Dropping

June 1947 — Norman Hansen at his office building watching jump practice. Is that really a cigar I'm smoking? (Yes)

From our office windows, we could see the DZ. We often kept an eye on the troopers coming down in training jumps as we worked, and it was interesting to watch them during breaks.

One day, we watched a stick of ten come out, and nine chutes opened. The tenth did not open—it came straight down. *Bam!* One guy in the office immediately got on the phone to the Drop Zone and had to know, "Was somebody killed?" No, it was just some cargo they tossed out. Whew!

Flying Boxcar Demonstration

The history of parachute jumping in the military goes all the way back to the time of the horse cavalry and continues to the use of helicopters in the present day (2018). The basic tenet is to develop highly mobile fighting units. At the time of this story, the army was experimenting with using large airplanes to move troops and material. Large airplanes? The C-82, nicknamed "the flying box car," was capable of transporting tanks!

To that end, the 11th Airborne Division (Rear) prepared a demonstration of capabilities on May 12, 1947. This was a widely orchestrated visit that brought a large number of people to the base. In a handout to welcome visitors (I read "brass"), Major General Joseph May Swing said, "You will be given the opportunity to observe... parachutes, gliders and equipment containers." The entire handout for the big event was:

The primary purpose of your visit to the 11th Airborne
division is to witness the Airborne air-transport
capabilities of the latest type C-82 troop carrier
aircraft. This demonstration is sponsored by Headquarters
Army Ground Forces in conjunction with Army Air Forces.
In addition to the instruction on the latest type troop
carrier aircraft, it is planned to give you an opportunity
to observe certain aspects of airborne training and
equipment. This will be accomplished by arranging a few
days tour at the Division Airborne School where you will
have an opportunity to observe the individual training
and equipment necessary to produce a qualified
parachutist. You will also be given the opportunity to
observe certain equipment common to an airborne division;
such equipment will include parachutes, gliders and
equipment containers.

During your brief stay at Camp Schimmelpfenning, it is
my desire that you be afforded every opportunity to make
your visit as comfortable and enjoyable as possible.

WILLIAM M. MILEY

Asst. Div. Comdr.

May 1947 – Handout produced under direction of General Swing.
The typo in the camp's name was in the original handout.

All of this leads up to my participation in the demonstration event.
They asked for volunteers to make a parachute jump on display, and I
needed one final jump to maintain my status as a parachutist.
Therefore, on a brisk May morning in Camp Schimmelpfennig, a
group of ten, including myself, boarded the "Toonerville Trolley" to
Yamoto. There, we were issued parachutes and harnessed up. After
an hour or so, we were loaded into the C-82 "flying boxcar" cargo
plane.

Paratroopers jump from C-82 Packet in training exercise.
Photo by U.S Airforce

This airplane had twin booms. Cargo and personnel were loaded and unloaded into the body of the plane between them. There followed a short flight to the drop zone. It was chilly in the plane, and we were wearing harnesses so tight that we could barely stand up. We circled the drop zone for nearly an hour, all the while watching the red smoke indicators in the DZ showing ground winds too strong for safety. To our disappointment, the jump was called off.

My Samurai Sword: Now You See It, Now You Don't

The G-4 office where I worked was in charge of supplies and equipment. This included captured Japanese equipment such as vehicles, manufacturing equipment, dynamos (electric generators) and, yes, Samurai swords.

One day Captain Lumpkin told me to get a Jeep from the motor pool and take it into Sendai to fetch a certain sword expert and an interpreter, which I did. Following instructions, I took the two men back into camp and into a storage building, where a musty, dust-smelling, padlocked loft held several hundred Samurai swords. Using a key given to me, I unlocked the room and saw the swords laid out in a glittering array. The sword expert, under instructions from our interpreter, chose the ten best swords and laid them out on a separate table. Then he identified each of the swords by maker(s), age and ownership. The top three swords were set aside to become gifts to superior officers. The benefit of rank in the military was much like in civilian life.

When I reported back to the Captain he said, "Hansen, would you like a sword?"

Would I? Wow! What a terrific opportunity. I immediately went back to the loft and after considerable thought, chose what had been judged the tenth best sword. One big advantage was that it was short and would fit crosswise in the bottom of my foot locker. It shimmered in the bright sun and was simply beautiful. According to the information sheet alongside it, the sword was over 600 years old. The well-known makers of the sword were listed: who fashioned the hilt, who made the blade, who tempered the steel and so forth.

It transpired that when returning to the States, my duffel bag was not inspected, so there would have been no trouble bringing it home. So, where is the sword today? Hey, I was nineteen years old and could not resist showing it off and bragging about it. The following surprise inspection should not have been a surprise. So, it was no surprise that a Second Lieutenant confiscated the sword. I sincerely hope that he fulfilled my ultimate intention: to return this family heirloom to its original Japanese family.

"Abe" and the Dam Dynamo

It wasn't until "Abe" came to me with a proposal that I became aware that the army had confiscated a large electric generator suitable for a hydroelectric power plant. "Abe" was the only name given to me. He was a well-dressed, middle-aged man who took pains to inform me that he was a Christian. As it so happened, the company he worked for was vitally interested in that large dynamo. I think he was trying to "get the camel's nose under the tent," i.e., to get some sort of "in" with G-4 by cultivating contacts with some of the troops.

His proposal was that two evenings a week, he would take me to the home of his company's CEO, where I was to teach English to his seventeen-year-old son. In return, he would teach me Japanese. Unfortunately, I was too immature to recognize the opportunity and see the advantage. Sometimes, I wonder about what direction my life might have taken had I been a bit more grown-up. The CEO *might* have had an attractive, interesting daughter. Who knows?

I never did find out if the company received the dynamo.

USS Hollister

In June of 1947, as I recall, the Navy visited Sendai with their new destroyer, the *USS Hollister*. The big ship came into port, and they said they had room for two more soldiers to ride along as guests. They were very democratic about choosing people in our offices. They could have just picked from the officers, but we drew straws and a lieutenant and I won.

June 1947 — Soldiers tour the ship before the USS Hollister departs. JD Owen is on the left and Edel the Beetle is seated on the right.

June 1947 — Army barge with sailors headed out to USS Hollister.
Barge's insignia is "US Army 4C-11"

We boarded the destroyer at Sendai that afternoon and went out to sea. The plan was to make a shake-down cruise from Sendai to the north end of Honshu Island at Aomori.

June 1947 — Looking shoreward as the USS Hollister leaves Sendai Bay. The small craft is approaching to pick up the bay pilot.

June 1947 – The small craft departs after picking up their bay pilot.

June 1947 — The captain takes a sighting on the USS Hollister.

I stood beside the captain and borrowed his binoculars while they had gunnery practice! They would fire the five-inch guns out to sea, making a big boom and belching a black cloud of smoke far off in the distance. Their 20 mm and 40 mm guns were equipped with every third or fourth round as a tracer so they could see where they were shooting. The gunnery practice consisted of firing at the big black clouds out at sea. We watched the tracers as they "hit" the big black cloud. This was extremely noisy and quite impressive.

June 1947 — The prow of the USS Hollister with one five-inch gun in the center, bracketed by (I think) 40 mm guns.

I happened to turn shoreward and look away from the target practice. All the Japanese fishing boats were headed for shore just as *fast* as they could possibly go! They probably thought the war had broken out again, and I can't say I would blame them. It really was awfully noisy.

*June 1947 — Norman Hansen briefly borrows a
Navy cap from friendly sailors*

The Navy really "put on the dog" and served an excellent steak dinner with all the trimmings to its guests. They were gracious hosts, and we had a taste of how Navy life could be. The *USS Hollister* docked at Otaru, near Aomori. Because they fed us so well, we jokingly suggested that we were in the wrong branch of service.

June 1947 — Norman Hansen on the USS Hollister

On arrival, we left the ship and rode an overnight train to return to Sendai. On this leg of the trip, I became aware of how very mountainous Japan was. Looking out the train window, I saw mountains everywhere and rice paddy terrain on the hillsides.

June 1947 – Launching the lifeboat in preparation for a drill

June 1947 — Lifeboat drill on the USS Hollister

June 1947 — The main guns

June 1947 — Captain's view from the upper bridge

June 1947 — USS Hollister bridge

June 1947 – Returning to land at the harbor at Otaru
after our "luxury cruise"

June 1947 — Left to right: Norman Hansen on the USS Hollister with LeRoy Edel and John Werner

June 1947 – USS Hollister, as we left her docked in Otaru after our two-day trip from Sendai. Photo taken on 35 mm Mercury II camera by Norman Hansen.

Soldiering

Walking Mattress Covers

October 1946 — Troops in formation outside our barracks in Camp Schimmelpfennig, Sendai, Japan. Envision these barracks painted with a nice, light, bright blue. These troops have "fallen in" and are in formation, ready for inspection or marching.

You may have noticed that our office crew's duties were really more like an ordinary job and not very soldier-like. Indeed, that was so.

The only real soldiering we did was in basic training and parachute training. Others, the "real soldiers," were required to "fall in" formation before breakfast for roll call and inspection. They were required to be in complete uniform, shaved, clean and ready for the day. To my way of thinking, avoiding the daily inspections was a big advantage.

On rare occasions, however, we had to "fall in" for inspection. "Falling in" meant lining up on the parade ground in a specified order with a sergeant in front. Needless to say that early in the morning, our group was a pathetic sartorial excuse for "real soldiers." Caught unexpectedly, many were not yet shaved or completely dressed.

Our sergeant was a Master Sergeant, and he had mastered a truly impressive pejorative vocabulary. It was surprising how long he could rant and rave without repeating himself. A couple of the epithets he employed stick in my mind, but they didn't actually mean anything to us, because at the command "Fall out!" we cleaned up, had breakfast and went off to work again as usual. Some of his favorite phrases were, "Youse bunch of walking mattress covers!" and, "You slimy afterbirth of a dead mule!" To have experienced the skill this sergeant displayed expressing himself while "chewing out" the troops was a real treat. The guy was an artist.

Too Many Mattresses

In the barracks, there were extra mattresses at times. Army mattresses were thin and rather firm. When there was room after people had left, and the barracks weren't completely full, some of us would take the extra mattresses and put two or more on our bed. At one point in time, I had *seven*! But it was too difficult to make the bed and really not very comfortable. Besides, I could still feel a pea placed under the bottom mattress, even through the seven stacked on top of it.

At the head of each bed in the barracks and against the wall was a tall, gray metal locker. It had a rod for hanging clothes and shelves for mess kit, shoes, etc. At the foot of each bed was a foot locker—a hinged box on a stand to hold underclothes, socks and so forth, along with personal belongings.

Batman

I had a Japanese batman, a man forty-one years old, who took care of my clothes, did my laundry, made the bed and so forth. I paid him a carton of cigarettes a week, which cost me about sixty-five cents, if I remember correctly. He worked for several troopers in the barracks. I'm sure he re-sold the cigarettes and made really good money. He could get 350 yen for them, and 100 yen equaled about $2.00.

March 1946 — Takahashi and "Papa San" seated. Papa San is wearing a vest. This is the back corner of our office building.

My Water Gets Turned Off

I was standing at the urinal in the men's restroom relieving myself when a three-star general stepped up to the urinal next to me. There was only one three-star general on base, Lieutenant General Joseph May Swing and he was legendary. Indeed, I was wearing some clothing by his design; the cap on my head was called the Swing Hat.

We somewhat affectionately called it the "cunt cap" due to its suggestive appearance.

"Good morning, son," he said. Being nineteen, green as grass and awed by the brass, my stream shut itself off. "Good morning, Sir," I mumbled, zipped up, washed up and dashed out.

Pissing Contest

Some of us were country boys, some of us were city boys and all of us were just boys. So, when the snow came, there came also jokes about yellow snow; such as:

Two men walking home from work saw, in the snow by the house written in yellow, "Joe Loves Mary." The one man began cursing angrily. "I don't see why you're angry, I think it is kind of cute," said the second man. "I would too, but that is Mary's handwriting!"

At any rate, somebody suggested that we see who could leave their yellow mark out the farthest distance. We took turns and had two tries each. It was no contest. John Werner muscled his stream out more than a foot beyond anybody else's. Boys will be boys.

February 1947 – Wide expanse of snow, shown here around the A-G Rear building, simply waiting for someone to write on it.

When Things Go Wrong

A Dip in the Rice Paddy

It transpired that Chief Warrant Officer Harold Lloyd had gotten a new camera, and he wanted a lieutenant from his office to take his picture. They were in the rice paddies. The lieutenant stood in one place, looking into the viewfinder and said, "Back up a little, will you, Chief? You're too close."

And Warrant Office Lloyd said, "No, I'm on this little knoll, you back up."

So, the lieutenant backed up, not realizing there was a "honey bucket" or cesspool pit directly behind him. The next thing we knew, the lieutenant was in over his head in a pit full of human waste. All you could see was this hand poking up, holding the camera. He saved the camera! (I sure wish I had that on video!)

We came close to losing Warrant Officer Lloyd—he almost died laughing!

*October 1946 — Chief Warrant Officer Harold Lloyd
in G-1 Personnel, holding his camera*

February 1947 — Picture of rice paddies, taken from on the train to (or from) Yamoto before (or after) jump training. The straight, white lines are raised walkways separating each rice paddy.

Airstrip Tragedy

August 1947 — An L-14 on dirt runway behind my office building in Camp Schimmelpfennig, Sendai.

We saw a terrible thing. Our office was right at the eastern edge of Camp Schimmelpfennig. Beyond the fence just outside our office was an airstrip where two or three little Cub airplanes, an L-14 or a similar model, took off and landed a few times daily.

One day, a young Japanese man pulled the chocks out of one front wheel and ran around to the other wheel. He could not see the spinning propeller and ran right into it. That was it. He never knew what hit him. One moment he was there, and the next he was gone. Ruined his whole day. Ruined our day, too. We had to do an awful lot of work and keep busy to try to handle the trauma.

Thanksgiving in Jail

*February 1947 — The captain's jeep at Camp Schimmelpfennig,
similar to the one that put Norman in jail.*

I have always considered myself a law-abiding citizen, but sometimes circumstances change appearances. It was the day before Thanksgiving Day in 1946 when Captain Conner of G-3 (Operations) was transferred from Camp Schimmelpfennig to headquarters in

Sapporo. He gave me the keys to his Jeep and charged me with the task of shipping the Jeep by rail on the following Monday. The temptation was too great for a nineteen-year-old boy, and on Thanksgiving morning, Clancy and I went for a "short joy-ride." I did not notice the "One Way" sign down a Sendai alley, but the MPs did and pulled me over. Unfortunately, even though I was in charge of managing the motor pool, I had no proof I had not stolen the Jeep, and we soon found ourselves behind bars. It was very embarrassing and hard to do, but, shame faced, I called Captain Lumpkin and confessed my sins. Clancy and I "enjoyed" our turkey dinner behind bars before Captain Lumpkin came to vouch for us. He was obviously and rightly irritated and disappointed. When I first started work with the Captain, his present clerk, a staff sergeant, spent the week before he shipped out teaching me my duties. I believe this shenanigan (and others) kept me from being promoted beyond corporal. Well, maybe, but I have no complaints.

When Hygiene Fails

I have always considered myself a person with habits of cleanliness. Apparently, there are degrees of cleanliness, as the doctor explained while examining the large ripe boil that had erupted in the middle of my body just under my belt buckle. When you sweat and the belt traps that and rubs against it, bacteria will find a good spot to propagate. Or, quite possibly, friction from the belt caused an ingrown hair which had become festered.

I explained my problem, and he asked me to dress down and lay on the examining table. Laying on my back with my midriff exposed, he lanced the boil. To my surprise, it did not hurt; the pressure relief felt good. He cleaned the pus out of a quarter-inch hole and then used a Q-tip to soak up any remaining moisture. I was lying there in the office with the Q-tip sticking up out of my stomach. I wondered what people thought as they walked by.

I Quit

In my later years, I have come to the conclusion that using tobacco is a form of failure in personal hygiene. Unfortunately, the military services in the 1940s practically endorsed cigarette smoking by making their purchase so inexpensive. During training exercises, it was common for the Sarge to say at break time, "Smoke 'em if you've got 'em."

Most of our office staff did not smoke. JD Owen smoked, but he wanted to quit. So, as an incentive, he gave me 200 yen and said that if he smoked anytime during the next month, I should keep the money. I am sorry to say that the power of addiction won out and my college fund was 200 yen (about $7) richer.

I confess that my personal hygiene failed at times. I enjoyed an occasional cigarette or cigar. I did not really "get hooked" until after I was out of the service. I got myself "unhooked" on January 1st, 1990, when I quit cold turkey and was ever after a 100 percent non-smoker.

Sinus Trouble

Not everything was fun and games. One night, I woke up in the middle of the night to discover that I was crying in my sleep. My face hurt so bad that sleep was impossible.

As soon as I could, I went on sick call. The doctor, a nice-looking young man who looked like he had just graduated from medical school, diagnosed a sinus problem. He then proceeded to ream my sinuses with a cotton swab on the end of a wire—without any topical anesthetic or pain killer. This procedure hurt so much that I gripped the chair's Bakelite arms and gasped, "No, No!" On a pain scale of one to ten, that had to be at least a nine.

After a year or so of this torture, he finally finished. Unfortunately, it was all in vain.

The next day, I tried the dentist, where X-rays revealed an impacted wisdom tooth. I wish I had been wise enough to visit the dentist first.

The dentist, a young naval officer, like the doctor, did not look old enough to have a degree. He gave me a shot to numb the pain, then fussed around a little and approached my mouth with a needle and thread.

"What's that for?" I asked.

"Well, I had to cut open the gums to get at the tooth to extract it," he replied.

I had not even felt him do any of that. What a difference in pain management (mismanagement?)! His pliers did the trick; I immediately felt much better and recovered quickly.

Our Screw-Up

Every outfit seems to have their "screw-up." You know, the one who can't seem to do anything right. I will call ours McGrunty, although it's not his real name.

McGrunty never did seem to develop functional listening skills. This became very evident during parachute training. Our sergeants stressed, over and over, that when descending from a parachute drop, you should *keep your eyes on the horizon!* It was clearly explained this was the best way to calculate distance to the ground. Also, looking straight down was dangerous because of human nature: When seeing the ground rush toward you, instinct calls for you to pull your legs away from the danger. On his first jump, McGrunty looked down, pulled up his legs, landed on his tailbone and broke his back.

He got the same health lectures as the rest of us, but he could not stay away from the Japanese women nor be bothered to use prophylactics. The result? Syphilis. In his case, sadly, incurable syphilis. This is a devastating and painful disease. In the barracks one night, he woke me and asked me to go with him to sick call for a shot against the pain. He'd been moaning and keeping us awake, so I knew the only way to get any sleep was to help him out. We woke an unhappy orderly who grunted, "You again! Drop your drawers." The orderly then filled a needle with medication, slapped one rump quite smartly and injected the other.

Later, shortly before McGrunty died, he provided lessons to others about the importance of making good choices. He was put on stage, behind curtains, with his ugly, chancre-covered penis sticking out between the drapes. The troops had just finished watching a film on venereal disease. Then, upon leaving the theater, every soldier had to march by for a close-up look.

After that, I don't see how any soldier could go out and consort with a Japanese woman for hire.

Food and Drink

Too Many Eggs

One of Captain Lumpkin's jobs was as mess officer. One day, he said, "Hansen, is there anything you think the troops would like? I have no idea what they really want."

This was my golden opportunity! "Well, Sir, for my part I would like more eggs," I suggested.

"OK," he responded, "I will increase egg consumption to one and a half eggs per day, per man."

These eggs were reconstituted from powder and, other than as ingredients in cooking, were always served scrambled. I soon tired of the excess of powdered eggs, having grown up on a farm with fresh eggs daily. But I was afraid to mention it to Captain Lumpkin. He would probably ask me for more advice.

I learned to be careful of what to ask for: You might get it!

Officer's Locker Fund

That there was such a thing as the "Officer's Locker Fund," I was totally unaware until Captain Lumpkin invited me to participate.

"You ante up $20 in U.S. (not script) and, in return, after about a week or so you will receive all the hard liquor that it will buy."

I decided to gamble on it. It never occurred to me that this booze was purchased before government taxes were imposed. Imagine my surprise when I was delivered *ten* bottles—lots of whiskey, some vodka and some gin. Most of it, I sold to the troops in the barracks for $15 to $20 a bottle. More money to send home for college.

We worked Saturday mornings in exchange for Wednesday afternoons off. It seemed fitting to share my good fortune with my Saturday afternoon pinochle-playing pals, Bob Watson, LeRoy Edel and Krause (the Mouse). After lunch, we set up the card table in the office. We enjoyed using our ready supply of Cokes for mixers and chasers, and we quietly worked our way through two bottles of whiskey and opened the third. Having been well fed and sitting around the whole time, we thought that we were sober until Edel (the Beetle) got a really top-notch pinochle hand. He suddenly threw his cards straight up in the air and screamed, "Whee!" When we started moving about, we all discovered that we'd had *much* more to drink than nineteen-year-old boys could handle.

It was all downhill from there. We stopped drinking, but it was too late. We got sick, found a new use for our helmets and never repeated the experience.

Our pinochle games saved many a rainy Saturday afternoon. We did not play the version called "race horse"—that is, we did not pass cards, but played the hand we were dealt. Bidding began at 150 and seldom did bidding go very high. I mention it here only because of one very unusual hand. I can vouch for the honesty of the deal, for I dealt it. The cards were distributed and my partner, Krause the

Mouse, finally took the bid. He promptly laid down his meld of a run in spades: A, 10, K, Q, J, 9. Then a strange look came over his face. "Hey," he said, "I have another run in spades!" And down came another A, 10, K, Q and J. He was missing the other 9 of spades, but that's okay, he held an ace of diamonds. The odds of this pinochle hand occurring must be astronomical.

Beware the Sake

This one guy was hitting the sake pretty heavily over the weekend. He lived upstairs in the barracks, and on Sunday morning, when he didn't wake up, a bunch of us got hold of his cot. He didn't notice while we carried his bed down stairs and out the door. When he woke up at about 10:30 in the morning, he found he was out in the parade ground, bed and all! He was shocked and very surprised, but his buddies helped bail him out.

Drinking alcohol was a popular pastime, but resources were limited. The guys in our offices were, at most, casual drinkers. Beer was available in the day-room, which offered a couple of pool tables. The local beer was quite good.

Some of the men in the barracks would buy sake (rice wine) on the street, rather than from a reputable shop. On a Saturday, a trooper from our barracks obtained a large glass jug of sake, perhaps two or three liters, and sipped happily at it all afternoon and evening. The next day, Sunday, around 11am, his friends woke him up to enjoy the sunshine streaming through the window. "What sunshine?" he asked, "it's still dark." When they figured out that he had lost his vision, they urged him to go on sick call. He refused, saying, "I'll go on Monday." Then Monday morning came and so did his vision, but what an object lesson to everyone. He was one badly frightened, miserable individual for a day, and very fortunate to recover completely.

Cold Coca-Cola

1947 — Container, Round, Insulated M-1941
Image courtesy of C.E. Daniel Collection

We had a Coca-Cola bottling plant in camp. In the office, we kept our Coke bottles cool in ice in a seven-gallon "Container, Round, Insulated, M-1941," usually called a "mermite" container. This can, a cooler which the army used for food and medical supplies and other things, was a good place to keep your Cokes cold. Mermite cans were made of metal, shaped like a round tin can. They were about cans were made of metal, shaped like a round tin can. They were about twelve to eighteen inches in diameter and just over one foot tall. Ours were painted red.

Norman took a college correspondence course in Algebra. Here, he is reading a book named "College Algebra." The clock reads 5:41pm, and there is an empty bottle of Coke on his desk.

We bought Cokes for five cents apiece, which matched what they charged us at the bottling plant. I'd get up in the morning and go over to the office. I could drink coffee in those days, but instead I'd drink a dime's worth of caffeinated Cokes before breakfast.

Everybody paid for their Cokes, and there was always enough money to buy more. We helped ourselves to a Coke whenever we wanted and were expected to pay five cents per bottle in military script. Periodically, this money was used to refill the mermite cooling can with more bottles of Coca-Cola. The mess hall let us have all the ice we needed.

Sample of my military script used on the army base in Sendai

I grew up in a rural area on the northern edge of Seattle, where our cows produced milk. I was accustomed to fresh, whole milk every day. In Japan, I discovered that I couldn't abide the reconstituted "chalk-water" served as milk in the mess hall. I was young and not a coffee drinker, so I substituted Cokes. Every morning before breakfast, I went to the office and drank a Coke or two. At 8am when office duty started, I would have my next Coke out of my three or four for each day.

Coke was bottled in eight-ounce green glass bottles. The bottles were imported from the States and often had the state of origin embossed on the bottom. We soon enjoyed studying the bottles closely, looking for these stamps, as they gave us feelings of connecting with home.

Before joining the army, when I was seventeen in 1944, I made my first visit to the dentist and was told, "You have no cavities." Returning home in 1947 at age twenty, I had my second dental appointment. The fillings from this visit cost over $200, which was a great deal of money at the time and used up most of my college savings. That amount of work would probably cost a few thousand dollars today in 2016.

I tried to figure out what could cause the sudden damage in my mouth. I soon discovered that the pH of Coca-Cola was around 2.7. This is quite acidic and probably accounted for all the dental problems, as the acid ate away at the protective enamel.

Some teachers do a science fair demonstration with teeth. When I was a public-school teacher and one of the kids lost a tooth, I would ask, "When the tooth fairy is done, can you bring it in to class?" We'd pour a glass of Coca-Cola and drop the tooth into the glass to demonstrate what happens. Within a week, the acid in the Coke would have eaten off much of the tooth's enamel. The outside of the tooth became soft to the touch.

Are you listening, kids? Or are you going to prove Benjamin Franklin's saying: "Experience keeps a dear school, but fools will learn in no other."

Camp Life

How did the troops spend their leisure time? Following are some examples of how the office crew and I would enjoy our off-duty time.

Diving into the Deep End

In the summertime, the swimming pool was heated. The pool itself was quite large. At the deep end were two diving boards. Our work in the office gave us Wednesday afternoons free in exchange for working Saturday mornings.

Several times on a Wednesday, my close buddy Clancy and I had the swimming pool to ourselves. I had always wanted to be able to do a one-and-a-half forward somersault. I became determined that here was my chance to learn. I made several swan dives off the 3-meter board to accustom myself to the height. Then, telling myself how tough paratroopers were, I launch myself into the air and spun forward into a somersault. Unfortunately, I had managed only one-and-a-quarter revolutions and did, I was told, a beautiful spinning belly flop. Ouch!

Before I chickened out, I tried it again with only slightly better results. On the third or fourth try, I was able to rotate enough to enter head first. My stomach looked and felt like it was the recipient of a severe sunburn. Years later, at the University of Washington, I took a diving class and mastered that flip off the low board.

Rent-a-Horse

*August 1947 – Norman Hansen and Bob Watson at
the army's horse paddock*

Camp Schimmelpfennig was well organized to ensure free time did
not have to be boring. Most facilities were on the post, but at least

one—horseback riding—was on the beach in Sendai, an easy walk from camp. Here, at a riding academy, non-commissioned officers (enlisted men in the grade of corporal or above) were entitled to a horseback ride at no cost. Our gang, four or five of us, took advantage of this and had some fun rides along the beach. I remember looking out over the Pacific Ocean and thinking, "About 3,000 miles in that direction is home!"

The horses were rental horses and accustomed to all levels of riding experience. Though I was not an accomplished rider, it helped that I grew up with horses. My family had horses at home, but I was never a great horse person. I'd ridden them now and then, but my older brother Roald and sister Merna were serious riders.

Some riders had to stay within a corral for fear of being dumped or the horse running off with them. One exciting incident occurred when Bob Watson was inadvertently given a Thoroughbred race horse. This time, instead of turning from the stables toward the beach, the horse turned the other way to the road and took off! Bob said afterward that it was all he could do to hang on. This valuable horse wanted to run, and it did. Flying along, reins in hand and wind in his hair, Bob became aware of a Jeep alongside pacing him. Eventually the horse tired, and Bob got the race horse back under control.

When he stopped, the Jeep did, too. The driver, a major, said, "I clocked you on my speedometer. Do you have any idea how fast you were going?"

"No, Sir," answered Bob.

"You were doing just over 35 miles per hour," said the major.

Bob was glad to get back safely without harm to the horse or himself. The groom that gave him that horse really got in trouble. He had made a grievous mistake letting that valuable horse out.

I thoroughly enjoyed our rides along the beach, shouting back and forth and splashing in the shallow water's edge on the ocean. I believe the horses enjoyed it, too.

Football Game

*November 1946 — Football stadium "Smith Field" in
Camp Schimmelpfennig*

For many years, I kept a copy of the *Stars & Stripes* newspaper with an article about a football game in Camp Schimmelpfennig in November of 1946 and a photo of the team. We could see the stadium from the upper floors of the barracks.

During this game, I was seated near two officers, one from 11th Airborne and the other from 8th Army. They each bet $50, a very large sum for the time, for their own team. The Airborne officer bet

$50 that Airborne would win by 50 points or more. Fifty points! I thought this was inconceivable.

As it turned out, the 11th Airborne officer won his bet by half time. Again, inconceivable. It seems that the Airborne division had attracted quite a number of top athletes, and some of them were top-ranked college football players.

Oh yes, I did enjoy the game, even after it became boring. Final score: 93 - 0.

Japan League Football Article

This photo and article about their astonishing success is reproduced from the *Stars & Stripes* clipping from my archives:

THE DEFENDING CHAMPS—Pictured here are the members of the 11th Airborne Angels' first string eleven. The Angels are currently leading the American Football League of Japan and seem assured of capturing their second consecutive loop championship. (° °ng Photo)

November 1946 — Newspaper photo from the Stars & Stripes article

Angels Heading for Japan League Title

By PFC Bernard Kaplan, Staff Writer

"The mighty 11th Airborne Angels, need little introduction, least of all to the members of the American Football League of Japan who have faced this pulverizing gridiron machine thus far during the season.

The Angels, defending champions, haven't tasted defeat in two years and at the rate they are traveling there isn't a team in the league who can pose a threat to their title aspirations.

These gridiron goliaths have played four games and in the course of play they have amassed the astonishing total of 217 points and at the same time held the opposition to a negligible 12 points.

Tom Mesereau's T-formation wizards have run up scores against all opposition that would require the use of an abacus for quick calculation. Airborne opened up its season with a 61-6 trouncing of Kobe Base and followed that up with a 43-6 rout of the Eighth Army Chicks. First Cavalry was the next victim succumbing 20-0. Last week, the gridiron heights were scaled when poor little IX Corps was literally stampeded as the Angels steamrolled to a 93-0, point and a half per minute score.

The Airborne eleven is styled after the Army T, ably tutored by head coach, Major Tom Mesereau, a West Point grid star in the class of '43. Assisting coach Mesereau are Lts. R. V. Newman, a Mississippi State luminary, "Ripper" Collins, from West Point, and Mike Kosonovich.

Although the Angels are faced with redeployment problems, they are more fortunate than the rest of the teams in the loop, insasmuch as they have a host of past, current, and future college stars in both the line and the backfield.

Add speed and physical conditioning to the experience and coaching that this club had on hand and you have the reason for 11th Airborne's success. These essential attributes when combined as they have, seem to warrant the assumption that there is nothing in sight that can stop the Airborne's championship march for the second year in succession.

The first team lines up with Gale Welch at left end and Eugene Roy at the opposite end post. Dan Wickline at 205 pounds is at left tackle and Ted Halligan, whom I first saw in action at Baker Field, New York with Red Blaik's first great Army team, smashes from the right tackle slot. Manning the guard posts are Trento Serine at left guard and a former Alabama star, Marion Edwards at right guard. Operating from the pivot post is Richard Kuh.

Quarterbacking this T-formation touchdown machine is Gene Roberts. Moving from left halfback is the former Oklahoma A&M speedster, Billy Grimes. Grimes is to the Airborne team what Glen Davis is to the Army eleven. Billy can truly carry the pigskin as every opponent faced can vouch. Charles Cooper is at the other wing back, and buttressing the backfield at fullback is James Phillips.

With a wealth of football talent backing up the first string, 11th Airborne once again is well on its way to establishing their gridiron supremacy."

Pro Bowlers

Our camp also had a six-lane bowling alley. Instead of automatic mechanical pin setters and ball returns, after each roll, a young Japanese boy would clear the deck and put the ball in a return rack. It was dangerous work, and Clancy and I, after paying for our games and shoe rental, would tip the pin setter a sum we thought was generous. It was customary for such workers to tend adjacent alleys, and this soon led to our quip to needle our buddies, "Set 'em up in the other alley!"

The bowling lanes were poorly maintained and we were soon getting lots of strikes, rolling the ball down what had become a dry groove leading to the strike pocket. Clancy Roberts and I decided we would have a forty-game contest over a period of time. This packrat has lost those score sheets since then, thank goodness. For those forty games, I averaged 239 and lost to Clancy's 240 average. We really thought we were good—maybe good enough to go on tour.

When I returned to the States, I went bowling at my first opportunity. You guessed it; I got scores in the 120s and 130s. Another day-dream bubble popped!

Field of Dreamers

March 1947 — Playing catch with Robert "Bob" Watson

Out behind our C-102 offices was an unused area, maybe one hundred feet wide, between our building and the fence. This spot became our "field of dreams" in the spring, when Robert produced a catcher's mitt and a baseball. Here we played out our baseball fantasies and became star major league pitchers and catchers. Anyhow, we got a lot of exercise and developed a wonderful camaraderie.

August 1947 – Playing catch with Leroy Edel

Boxing

Since I was in charge of the motor pool, occasionally some of the drivers would drop into the office for a chat. One of the drivers was a feisty young Latino who weighed just one hundred pounds and was on the boxing team. One day, while goofing off in my office, he said to me, "Hansen, hit me!"

"What?" I asked.

"I said to hit me!" he repeated. "I don't think you can," and he stood in front of me while I rose to the challenge.

I swung tentatively at first, but soon quite seriously. He was so fast, shifting and swaying that even if he did not move his feet, I couldn't touch him. I discovered why they liked him so much on the boxing team.

Daisy

1946 — Daisy enjoys the staff of building C-102

One does not really recognize the importance of having a pet until the situation precludes one. We all need to express affections and most dogs readily return the feelings. Daisy was no exception. Where or how Sergeant Fleishman came to have Daisy, I do not know, but he shared her with the rest of the office. Daisy never seemed to run out of loving affection, and she filled a much-needed niche. There seemed to be no limit to the amount of affection she could soak up and return. She was a very welcome addition to our office team.

1946 – Norman helping Daisy wave at the camera

Snow Skiing

Among a number of fun things that we did was to visit the Sakunami Ski Lodge one winter day, when four or five of us went skiing. The others of our group must have come from more affluent families. They all seemed to know what to do with skis on their feet. They went off by themselves while I stumbled around trying to figure this out for the first time.

Being a complete beginner, I naturally tried to ski down the beginners' slope. I had a terrible time. I finally realized that half of the problem of the beginners' slope was that it was so badly marred from all the spills that it was like trying to ski over moguls. I moved to the intermediate slope, and I could go swoosh from one side to the other. I could ski down the entire slope without falling! But I did twist a knee and it was pretty sore.

Fortunately, the ski lodge also featured the Sakunami Hot Springs with geothermally heated pools. The long, hot soak after skiing was ever so welcome. The feeling was even more enhanced by a hot toddy.

January 1947 — Sakunami Ski Lodge, Honshu, Japan

With prime facilities like these, it is easy to see how the Japanese could compete in the Winter Olympic Games and even host them in 1972.

Impressions of Japan

The Japanese People

Growing up in the Pacific Northwest, we encountered a number of Japanese people in daily life. Around Seattle, they had settled primarily in the Rainier Valley and the Vashon and Bainbridge Island areas. Right up until Pearl Harbor, they were known as neat, meticulous, hard-working and honest people. During World War II, they were all painted with the same brush: "Dirty, yellow-bellied Japs."

When I was sent to Japan with the Army of Occupation in 1946, the war had ended just over a year previously, and I wondered what kind of reception to expect. It did not take me long to decide that Japan's stance in World War II did not reflect the values of the Japanese people, but those of their political leaders back then. I found the Japanese people to be much like ourselves: mostly honest, friendly and approachable, with both "good guys" and "bad guys." Actually, living mostly at camp, I was pretty well sheltered from the local population, and thus experienced a minimum of culture shock.

Politically, the Japanese were in the throes of drastic change and were well on the way to adopting democracy. Hirohito, their leader who was considered an infallible god, publicly disclaimed the direction his country was heading. Under the leadership of General Douglas MacArthur, the country was making great changes and becoming an important ally.

In camp, I observed Japanese construction workers pause for lunch. Each man had a cloth-wrapped, rectangular tin. Curious, I gestured that I wanted to see what they brought to eat. One fellow unwrapped his tin, extracted a pair of chopsticks and held out his tin lunch bucket. To my surprise and horror, I saw a generous helping of fish heads and rice. He proceeded to eat it all and appeared to relish it.

Of course, their daily diet went well beyond this. I had little or no experience with Japanese cuisine, but recognized that besides rice, it included chicken, pork, beef, oriental veggies and lots of fish. It took me some effort to learn to handle chopsticks, and I still marvel at the Japanese chopstick dexterity. I know how they're supposed to work, but I can't get them to obey me.

Another cultural difference was the long history of the Shinto religion, whose devotees worship a large number of gods. According to modern *Wikipedia*, about 80 percent of the Japanese at this time espoused Shintoism. Many artistic shrines and edifices were erected for worshipping. General MacArthur issued the Shinto Directive in 1945, abolishing Shinto as a state religion and prohibiting some of its teachings and rites that were deemed to be militaristic or ultra-nationalistic.

I observed a number of other cultural differences. After all, this was the distant, exotic Orient—the Far East. They certainly did not dress like Westerners. Men did wear trousers, shirts, coats, hats and shoes, but the styles were different. You can guess that I find it hard to describe the differences. Note the formal garb of Hirohito in his famous photo with MacArthur on page 8.

February 1947 — Street vendors to illustrate fashion.
Note abacus at bottom left

It was my impression that women, at the time, were subservient to men and generally submissive. The women I encountered usually wore kimonos. Kimonos came in a wide variety of colors and styles, often containing silk embroidery of good quality and artistic value.

February 1947 — Tracks in the streets and shopping on the side

I've always remembered the Japanese girls in kimonos in downtown Tokyo. When they felt the urge, they would step off the curb over a street grating, squat down and a few moments later get up and walk away, all the while talking away with their friends. After adopting so many Western ways since then, I doubt that this practice prevails today, but I feel that there was something wholesome about avoiding false modesty. We are a product of our upbringing.

Japanese in general were very artistic and enjoyed art. Their art had a distinctly stylized and Oriental flavor that was easy to recognize.

As far back as the 1920s and 1930s, the Japanese were known for their ability to copy Western art and goods to export for sale. People believed then that this was their strength—copying. However, in art and manufacturing they have shown a great deal of innovation. For instance, although we took great pride in the quality of our warplanes, the Japanese "Zero" was deemed superior by those in the know.

Japanese music exposed me to distinctly different instruments and scales. I do not know enough about music to make judgements or comments. And, of course, their language was impossible—well, nearly. I did learn some phrases, and I can still count to ten and say "thank you" and "you are welcome" in Japanese.

Weather

Sendai in the wintertime had some gosh-awful rains and infrequent snow. Summer was not terribly hot. I'd say the weather was maybe a little warmer than Seattle in the summer and a bit cooler in the winter—and perhaps a little drier. Sendai is on the east coast and north of Tokyo.

We did get some snow in the winter and enjoyed snowball fights. Our barracks were a little more than one hundred yards from our offices and, during those "gully washer" rainfalls, we got pretty wet going to work in the morning. The offices were heated and we dried quickly.

All in all, the weather would be classified as temperate and reasonably comfortable for this boy from Seattle.

January 1947 — Snow is falling around the breezeway between two office buildings. Norman was a clerk in C-102. Behind the fence is a runway for small planes, then rice paddies and the drop zone.

January 1947 — Our daily walk between barracks and office is exposed to the weather

Stroll in the Park

In early spring of 1947, several of us had some leave time coming, so we took the train south to a large park. I do not remember the park's name, but it might have been Nara Park.

February 1947 — Park entrance and bus stop

February 1947 — Main entrance to the park

This particular park was filled with spectacular scenery and, judging from the monuments and statuary found, there was probably some religious background—possibly Shinto or Buddhist.

February 1947 — Monuments along the roadside while hiking to the top of the hill

Our main goal was to sight-see and get exercise. There were many fine sights to see and, being on a large hill, the paths offered plenty of walking up and down.

February 1947 — Monument of the war dead of the Sino-Japan War

There were many statues. We were especially attracted to a beautiful figure of an eagle with wings spread on top of a stone masonry tower about twenty feet tall. It was artfully and reverently made.

Apparently, the monument is in memory of those killed in the Second Sino-Japan War that had ended on September 9, 1937.

February 1947 — View from the hilltop of a bluff with a river that curves around Sendai

*February 1947 — A large clearing at the top of the hill
with monuments and a lion statue*

February 1947 — An army soldier "feeding" the lion

February 1947 — The life-sized stone lion statue was very detailed

A big clearing at the top of the hill offered views of the river meandering through the city and more statues. The concrete lion was just asking to be ridden or fed. I took some photos showing us enjoying this attractive statue.

February 1947 — Japanese children sit next to Norman as he visits the park. Note the traditional sandals.

Though it was a weekend, few Japanese families were on an outing, probably because it was still chilly. Language barriers disappeared when we interacted with the children. I am sure they were as curious about us as we were about them. They were neat, clean and very well behaved.

Coming down the hill while leaving the park provided some good views of the valley and a long steel bridge spanning the valley.

February 1947 — Note the long steel bridge spanning the valley over a meandering river. The bridge virtually radiates strength and beauty.

February 1947 — Looking down from the long steel bridge into the canyon.

This outing proved very entertaining, educational and esthetically pleasing. It is only now—in 2016—nearly seventy years later, that I began to wonder if we were acting like "ugly Americans" by disrespecting Japanese monuments. I wish I could visit these places again and see what remains today and how things have changed. Now who would have thought that a stroll through the park would bring such lasting and fond memories?

Mountains and Rice Paddies

Japan was beautiful—it really was. Our train trip from northern Honshu down from Sapporo to Sendai skirted a long, often snow-covered range of mountains and offered us views of spectacular scenery.

Rice was the critical staple crop necessary to feed the millions of Japanese. Given that the terrain was mostly mountainous, every bit of arable land had to be used. The rice fields came right up to the mountains and the edges of the roads, and the foothills were often terraced. Without amendment, the soil's fertility would soon deplete and rice production would decrease. A main source of fertilizer was human waste.

Outhouses were built up high enough to allow wooden barrels to be placed under the "holes." These barrels were beautiful, smooth and about three feet tall. The back of the outhouse had access to the barrels. Periodically, oxcart wagons would swap in empty "honey buckets" and take the full ones to a rice paddy. In one end of the rice paddy, a large hole was dug to receive the truly smelly contents. The human waste was allowed to compost until it was ready to spread onto the fields in time for setting out rice plants in the spring. This system worked for centuries, but I do not know if it is still in use today.

Japanese culture places a high value on beauty and harmony, so it seemed ironic that human waste made such an important contribution to the beauty and well-being of the country.

Black Market

Overall, the Japanese treated us very well, but I had a shock one time soon after I settled in. They told us we could sell our cigarettes on the black market. "Just go up-town, put a carton of cigarettes under your jacket and talk to somebody, and you can get a couple hundred yen— well over what you paid for it." The first deal I made went okay.

Then I went up-town and a gentleman came by, and asked, "How much?"

"Well," I said, "200 yen."

He said, "Just a minute," and went to get somebody that might have some money.

Two young, pretty Japanese girls came by; one looked up at me and said "Cigaretto! You and me and sister at my house, sleep all night!" About that time, an MP came around the corner. I hid the cigarettes and walked the other way. I never tried that again.

There was a thriving black market in camp, often fueled by GIs siphoning off goods meant for the troops. Trading on the black market could be very remunerative, but it came with the huge danger of getting caught. The army had no patience for these crooks, and the penalties were severe.

While in jump training at Yamoto, some of the cooks were selling food supplies meant for us on the black market. Half-jokingly, one soldier said, "I don't have to ask what is for dinner, just ask how the cabbage will be fixed." With our rigorous physical training, we did get very hungry. One night, all the troops in our Quonset hut shared the bounty when some of us broke into the storeroom and swiped bread and tropical butter. Yum! These cooks (actually crooks) were caught and paid the price.

Sex in the City

There were tea houses (read: bordellos) all over the city. In hard times, girls often sold themselves. Unfortunately, these girls were frequently exposed to STDs (sexually transmitted diseases) and were not safe partners. I steered clear of the prostitutes. Some of the fellows acquired gonorrhea and syphilis, and I didn't want any part of that. We received a chilling lesson when one of our men came down with incurable syphilis (see "Our Screw-Up" on page 111).

Sometimes, thinking I may have "missed out," I remember my many years of marriage, free from worry about re-occurrences of a disease or the prospect of transmitting such to a person I love. Now, I'm certain that I did the right thing.

Shopping

Tourists and servicemen going to a foreign country feel compelled to bring home mementos to remind them of the visit. I, certainly, was no different.

1946 — Typical shopping areas in downtown Sendai

*1946 — Another view of downtown Sendai,
including an air raid siren tower*

1946 — A Japanese tea trading company and photo studio

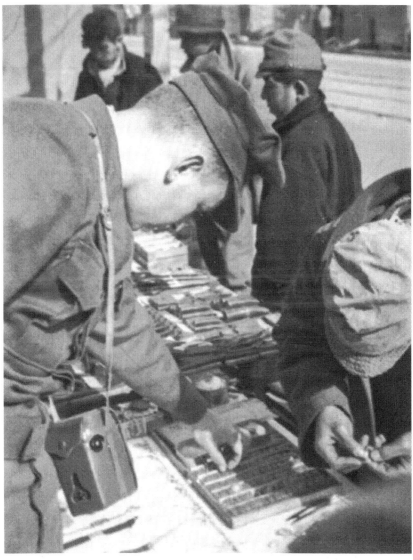

1946 — Hand crafted goods were an important local industry in downtown Sendai. You were expected to negotiate, but to be careful to not be too tight, for this was the sellers' way of making a living during very difficult times.

1946 — Street vendors displaying their ware in downtown Sendai

1946 — Stores and streets in Sendai

Photo processing shops were important because all photos had to be developed and printed in a chemical shop. Note phonetic spelling of "SERVISE," instead of "SERVICE."

Snake Ring

Silver ring in the shape of a snake

In 2015, about a year ago, I was exploring my box of mementos from Japan. My son Barry, standing by, was especially interested in some rings. One, a solid strip of silver, was coiled and made to resemble a snake, such as a cobra poised to strike. I don't remember exactly when I bought it, but it was from early in my time in Japan.

Being in my eighties at this time of writing, I decided to find it a good home with someone who admired it and cared about it. So, I gave it to Barry. That seemed such a good idea that I also gave him my two other solid silver rings: one of a skull (Happy Halloween, Barry) and the other an 11th Airborne insignia ring. These last two I bought at the PX (Post Exchange), a store in camp especially for servicemen. Barry also gratefully accepted my Japanese-made silver jump wings and glider wings. These were not official wings and were Japanese knock-offs (the back is stamped "Sendai 1946"), but were accurate in every detail. Today—in 2016—in online auctions, these knock-offs are considered very rare and command a hefty price.

I have always admired these, although I've never had a suitable occasion to wear them in public.

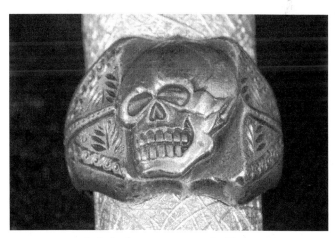

Solid silver souvenir skull ring

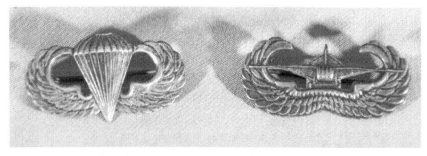

Silver paratrooper wings made in Sendai 1946 and glider wings

Sake Cups

A black lacquered tray holds golden yellow cups with red and black paintings of birds and branches.

In a souvenir store in downtown Sendai, I spotted an exquisite black lacquer tray about five-by-seven inches that held six hand-painted, thinly carved lacquered wood drinking cups. The paintings were on a golden colored background of plants and were very oriental in execution. Barry's youngest son, Daryl, studied Japanese in high school, so for his graduation, I gave him the sake cups and tray. It is my hope that he will treasure them and display them as the art objects they truly are.

Oil-on-Silk Painting

Japanese waterfall painting, oil on silk.

Daryl was gifted with my oil painting on silk of a Japanese waterfall. Here in the States, I had it beautifully framed and I enjoyed it on my wall for many years. It is possible (I think optimistically, even likely) that the painting could be or already is valuable. Anyway, I was (and still am) greatly enamored of it. The painting certainly epitomized the beauty of Japanese landscapes and the skill of Japanese artists.

Japanese Postage Stamps

Another item that may have value is the set of more than 100 Japanese postage stamps I bought in Sendai. Currently, they are part of my estate. These were originally packaged as, and sold as, souvenirs. Now, a good many of them are over one hundred years old. Again, postage stamps are works of art and the importance of the image and their rarity lend them value to collectors.

Over 100 Japanese stamps purchased in Sendai as souvenirs

Left to right: 1924 Empress Jingo, 1939 airplane over map of Japan, circa 1946 trading ship

Silk

Japan, for centuries, has been famous for its silk production. From my point of view, their offerings were of the best quality and yet were inexpensive. Besides some brightly colored silk handkerchiefs, a silk scarf (with Mary Lou's picture painted on an end), I once purchased six yards of sturdy silk with a pattern (which I now recognize as garish) of red-and-black half-inch squares. I sent this home to my mother who promptly sewed several silk shirts for the boys.

These shirts today are unfortunately--or perhaps fortunately--long gone, but the souvenirs did their job of reminding me of my visit to beautiful Japan.

In addition, I purchased some silk Japanese flags, one of them with the classic image of rays from the rising sun.

35 mm Camera

October 1946 — Norman's Mercury II camera bought in Japan from the Army PX for $35.

Perhaps my most useful souvenir was a Mercury II camera on sale at the PX. It advertised a "focal plane shutter" and it captured split frame photos from 35 mm film cartridges.

The focal plane shutter provided exceptional depth of focus. The split frame feature was very economical, as it delivered twice as many photos per roll since each negative image was half the usual size. I used this camera exclusively in Japan after I bought it. Almost all photos in this book came from this Mercury II camera. It now resides in Barry's collection.

I may be stretching the point a little by calling this a Japanese souvenir, because the camera was manufactured in New York. I bought it in the Army PX in Japan for $35.00. If the definition of a souvenir is something that reminds you of your travel, the camera fits it well, it being an important part of preserving memories of Japan.

Abacus

A Japanese abacus with an instruction manual that I purchased.

Cash registers were not a part of Japanese shopping. Instead, all clerks carried an abacus to calculate sales totals. The abacus, a set of beads on a framework, was widely used for mathematical calculations. I was very impressed to watch the store clerks' fingers flick the beads quickly this way and that. It reminded me of how a concert pianist could tickle the piano keys.

In 1946, mechanical adding machines and cash registers were common and had been around for some time. Back in 1890, for example, six years after John Patterson started NCR Corporation, 20,000 machines had been sold by his company alone. By 1900, NCR had built 200,000 cash registers, and there were more companies manufacturing them. Mechanical calculators dominated the desktop computing market through the 1960s. Many of these machines were designed for addition and subtraction by punching numbers on a big grid of buttons labelled 0-9 with a column for each place value, and some of them were driven by electric motors. Multiplication and division were done by repeated additions and subtractions.

There came a time when people wanted to know which was faster *and* more accurate: a calculator or an abacus. So, a contest was arranged between the two involving the best operators. It was held in the Ernie Pyle Theater in Tokyo. (Ernie Pyle was a famous war correspondent.) I don't recall what sort of adding machine was used, but it astounded many people when the abacus user dominated in adding, subtracting and multiplying, while coming close in division. I know, I was there.

Abacuses were not expensive, and I had to have one. I purchased the abacus shown in the photo above, and we still have it in the family to this day. In Japan, I learned its rudimentary usage but have forgotten most of it since then. To understand its basic premise, you need to know that each vertical column represents a place value: ones, tens, hundreds, etc. I used my abacus for teaching these concepts to sixth graders. A good abacus is a work of art; it's also very functional and, in some places, is still in use today.

USAHS Mercy

Yokohama to San Francisco

When they shipped us home a month before our enlistment was up, around late September or early October 1947, we first went to the replacement depot, the Repple Depot, in Yokohama. After a couple of days, we packed our duffel bags and boarded the *USAHS Mercy*, a hospital ship bound for San Francisco.

By then, I figured, "Oh boy, the Special Services is the way to go." I forget how I managed it, but I got to be head librarian—in fact the only librarian—in charge of the library. I was all set to sit around reading books and checking books in and out from Yokohama to San Francisco. Well, that lasted for two lovely days and someone caught on, or told on me, or pulled rank to get this position. They put me with the others chipping paint. Only two days of relaxing in the library—shucks! There is always painting to do on ships like that, and a hospital ship was kept as clean and sanitary as any on the seas. Crossing the Pacific Ocean was slow and uneventful—the best kind of voyage.

This was the fifth voyage for the *USAHS Mercy*, according to its souvenir newsletter. The ship had departed San Francisco on August 6th, reached Manila on Aug 28th, then Naha, Japan, on September 1st and Yokohama on September 5th, where it picked up quite a number of returning army troops, including me. We landed September 19,

1947. I'd been away from the USA for thirteen months and a few days.

September 19, 1947 — The Golden Gate bridge as seen from the troop ship USAHS Mercy, with soldiers returning from Japan.

It was amazing, coming on the hospital ship into San Francisco under the Golden Gate Bridge. From a distance, it looked like the ship couldn't *possibly* fit under that bridge. And when we got under it, I looked up, and it was way the hell and gone up above us. It was a glorious sight to see the good old USA again after a year overseas. Among the multitude of lessons learned was that I was very fortunate to be an American.

USAHS Mercy Newsletter

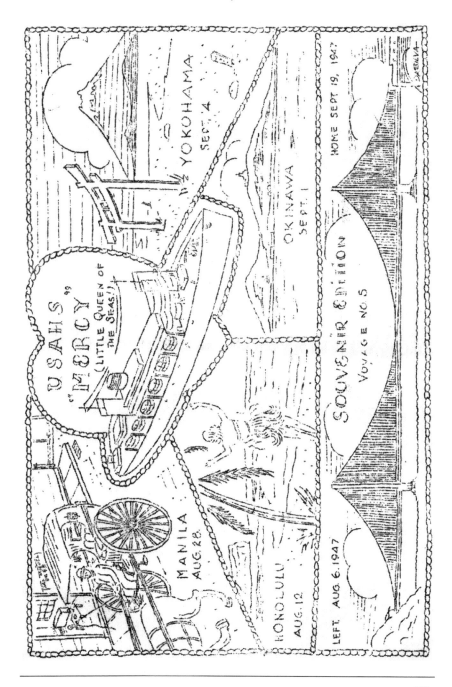

Crossing the Date Line

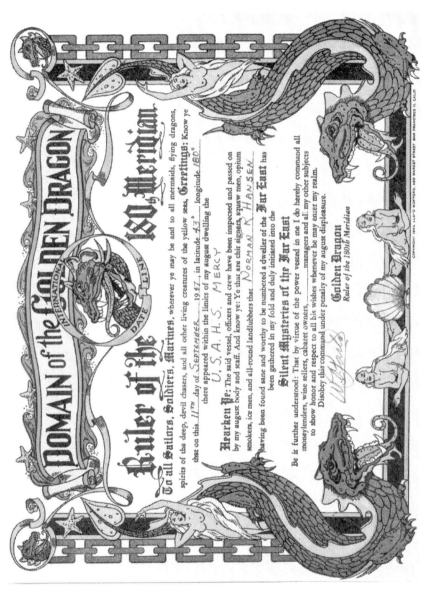

*September 11, 1947 – Certificate for crossing the International Date
Line, in colorful and salacious artwork.*

From San Francisco to Home

We arrived stateside in San Francisco and travelled to Camp Stoneman very near Oakland, but technically in Pittsburg, California. At this point, we were about to be discharged from the service and then travel home.

For travel pay to reach home, we were given a choice. They would pay us per mile to home or to the point of enlistment. Well, I had enlisted in Alabama which was much farther away from San Francisco than Seattle. So, I chose to get travel pay to Alabama, around $40 or $50, and used just $28 to take the bus home to Seattle.

I saved money while I was in the army. As a Paratrooper, we received $50 extra in jump pay each month. And I sent that home. The minor danger of jumping was worth $50 a month. Also, being overseas meant the basic pay was higher.

A couple of days at Camp Stoneman going through the process of becoming a civilian set me up for a long bus ride to Seattle and a short bus ride from Seattle to my family in Richmond Beach.

After warm greetings all around, I headed for the refrigerator and drank a quart of raw, whole cow's milk. *Aaaaaaah!* I had sure missed it.

Then I raided the cookie drawer. Not much had changed in the year I was gone.

The party was over. Now to go back to Real Life, a wiser, better prepared and all-around better person for the experience.

October 1947 – Corporal Norman Hansen, 20, at home in Richmond Beach. I'm about to go on a date, so I'm "dressed to impress" in the height of paratrooper fashion with pantlegs properly bloused and boots laced with white riser cord.

Epilogue

It was good for me to have experienced army life because I met a challenge. Here I was, nineteen and quite immature. I knew very little of the world. In the army, I met a lot of people from all walks of life and experienced a whole lot of different aspects of the world. I had a chance to grow up a little bit, gain some confidence and see a foreign country. I also developed an appreciation for our democratic way of life and felt I had a vested interest in our country. And yet, I confess to having very fond memories of Japan, the Japanese people and even army life.

I returned to the University of Washington, where the GI Bill paid for most of my college education, my savings paid for the rest and part-time jobs like being a "soda jerk" provided spending money. I was in a quandary as to choosing a major topic of study. Indeed, I felt completely lost as to what I wanted to do with the rest of my life, and I was facing a major decision point. The GI bill offered a test designed to identify your strengths and weaknesses as well as your main occupational interests. I was not surprised they reported I was well-suited for science, but somewhat surprised that they determined that being a teacher or pastor was suitable. I had always loved plants and gardening, so I chose Botany, began taking courses and I loved it.

I married Winifred Von Harten on September 10, 1949, and earned a Bachelor of Science degree in Botany in June of 1951. Then, I discovered I was not employable with simply a botany degree. Given stronger math skills, I could probably have gone into botanical research. Suddenly, I had an epiphany—why not become a teacher? I enjoyed—even liked—children, and with my wide variety of work and life skills, I believed I had something to offer. This began the next phase of my life: the push for a teacher's certificate while raising a family.

Because of my situation, I became acutely aware of the great benefits to our country of the GI Bill. Many ex-servicemen and women could become much better prepared to productively enter our country's workforce because of it.

I went on to work at a variety jobs while attaining my teaching certificate, which led to a long and rewarding career in the Shoreline School District teaching elementary school. We moved to Lake Forest Park in 1973 when Winnie and I became an "empty nest" family. I continued teaching until I retired in 1985. Winnie passed away from pancreatic cancer in 1995, and I was diagnosed with terminal cancer of the bile duct in February of 2016. (*Edit:* Norman passed away on August 17, 2016, and Barry purchased the property in Lake Forest Park from the estate.)

Now, as I write this seventy years after my experience as an army paratrooper in Occupied Japan in 1946 and 1947, I am warmly rewarded with this walk down memory lane and the opportunity to pass these stories down to my grandchildren and beyond. I love you all.

Norman Hansen

Appendix: 11th Airborne Division

The following sections are reproduced verbatim from handouts I received for a major base demonstration, in which I was to participate as a paratrooper on May 12, 1947. I'm reproducing this here for sake of completeness and for history buffs, since I wasn't involved very much in these events, other than the fact that my two older brothers Roald and Donald had already enlisted. The army's handouts include:

11th Airborne Division History

"The 11th Airborne Division was activated at Camp Mackall, N.C., on the 25th February 1943. It was the first of the airborne divisions to be activated, as such, for the 82nd and 101st were developed by a personnel split of the old 82nd Infantry Division. The 11th was then, and is now, commanded by Major General Joseph M. Swing.

Initially the table of organization provided for two glider and one parachute infantry regiments; two glider and one parachute F.A. battalions; one airborne engineer battalion and one airborne anti-aircraft battalion. The glider regiments were two-battalion units and all elements were considerably weaker, in man and fire power, than those of normal infantry divisions. Including its integral special units, the division's aggregate strength totaled 8,475 officers and men.

The infantry cadre of the glider units was drawn from the 76th and 88th divisions and the officer complement of the jump units from the parachute school and the airborne command. Filler replacements were assigned from the first eighteen-year-old draft.

By the end of 1943, all preliminary training phases were completed and on 1 Jan 1944 the division entrained for Camp Polk, Louisiana where it was subjected to a brief, but comprehensive, test maneuver. In February, the War Department authorized the division to establish its own parachute school and the organization of glider units was revised to require three quarters of their personnel to be qualified paratroopers.

On 7 April, the division began its movement to the staging area, Camp Stoneman, California and by 16 May all units had embarked for overseas shipment. The last of the division arrived at Oro Bdy, New Guinea, 12 June and a field camp was established at Dobodura Village, a few miles inland. During the next five months, the division completed its final pre-battle training which included unit tactical jumps, amphibious instruction, glider refresher training and jungle warfare problems.

The division embarked for the Leyte Operation, 5 November, and arrived at BITO Beach, 15 miles south of Dulag, on 20 November. Two days later it was committed with the mission of cutting the Japanese supply route along the line MAHONAG – ANAS – LUBI and effecting a junction with American elements operating in the ORMOC Corridor.

On 6 December, the division's special units were attacked by a Japanese parachute task force which jumped at 1840 and seized the SAN PABLO airstrip, near BIRAUEN. For several days and nights thereafter, it was paratrooper against paratrooper but the nip silk artists promptly joined their honorable ancestors.

Having taken the MAHONAG – ANAS – LUBI line and contacted the 7th division in the ORMO Corridor, the 11th closed the Leyte campaign, except for mop-up operations, on Dec 26th. On 25 January, it embarked for the Luzon campaign with the mission of securing a beach-head at NASUGBU, seizing strategic TAGAYTAY RIDGE – that rugged backbone ridge which separates Manila from the south. The two para-glider regiments were to move in, amphibiously, seize a foothold on the ridge and be reinforced, on D plus 4, by the 511th Prcht Inf., which was to make a "Vertical Envelopment."

At 0800, 31 January, the attack opened on schedule and by 1900 the division cleared phase-line eight, 24 hours ahead of schedule. The advance, however, was threatened by a huge, biscuit-shaped hill, MT. AIMING, which was heavily fortified and dominated by Highway 17, the only avenue of approach. At this time, General Swing decided to venture a night attack – one of the first to be launched in the Pacific Theater by Allied troops. At dawn, 1 February, this key terrain feature was taken although the Division absorbed a robust artillery shellacking while holding it.

On 3 February, the advance reached TAGAYTAY RIDGE and the object was secured when the 511th parachuted in and contact between the amphibious and jump echelons was gained. Thereafter, the division pushed on toward NICHOLS FIELD, on the outskirts of MANILA, where it was to meet its toughest opposition. The high ground around the field, and the field itself, was alive with nearly impregnable emplacements laced together with beautifully sited FPL's and backed up by plenty of artillery of all calibers. After suffering extremely heavy causalities, the division took this tough objective, 12 February, and moved to attack FORT MCKINLEY, in conjunction with the 24th Infantry and First Cavalry divisions. This operation ended, successfully, 17 February.

February 23rd, a combat team, consisting of the 1st Bn., 188th Para-Glider Inf., and the 1st Bn., 511 Prcht Inf., seized LOS BANOS PRISON, on the south shore of LAGUNA de BAY, liberated several hundred Allied prisoners and annihilated the jap garrison – at a cost of 2 killed and 2 wounded. We might have escaped the 4 casualties were it not for a Philippine woman collaborationist who "manned" a Jap .50 caliber machine gun with fair effect until silenced – peremptorily. The operation was well planned and coordinated and the parachute echelon, hitting the silk at dawn, caught the Nip garrison at morning calisthenics and 540 Japs were summarily liquidated. Sayonara – 'arui Des'!

After capturing TERNATE, on the southwest coast of Luzon, the division was ordered, in conjunction with Combat Team 158 and the 1st Cavalry Division, to attack and take the line ILIGAN – BATANGAS – LIPA – LINGA and on 23 March this operation ended successfully. The next objective was MT. MALEPUNYO which fell 4 May and the subsequent mop-up phase, concluded 5 June, was the division's final combat experience. It is credited with 187 days in action.

At the time of surrender, the 11th was on Okinawa undergoing training for the OLYMPIC operation which was to take Japan the hard way. Shortly thereafter, it was alerted for the air-move which was to inaugurate the occupation. Although the division does not claim to be the first American unit to arrive in Japan – that honor is shared by several small airborne engineer units – it air-landed on Atsugi strip on 29 August 1945 and garrisoned Yokohama until relieved by other ground-force troops. It was therefore the first combat division to reach the Land of the Cherry Blossom and the Honey Cart.

Since the end of the Luzon Campaign, the division's table of organization has changed considerably. It now provides for two parachute Infantry regiments, and a third glider F.A. Bn., (105's) has been added. The aggregate strength now authorizes 13,015 officers and men."

11th Airborne Division Training Center

The following description of the training center is reproduced verbatim from a handout for a demonstration to army brass on May 12, 1947:

"Shortly after the assumption of occupational duties in Northern Japan, Major General Joseph M. Swing, 11th Airborne Division Commander, directed that a school be organized to qualify as parachutists, replacement coming into the Division.

At the time, Yanome Airstrip, about 15 miles south of Sendai was the chosen site. On 24 November 1945, a cadre consisting of 15 officers and 38 enlisted men under the command of Capt. Peter J. Eaton arrived at Yanome prepared to organize the 11th Airborne Division Jump School.

On 2 December 1945, the first class consisting of 200 students reported for training. Class number 1 made its first training jump on 10 December 1945 and its qualifying jump on 16 December 1945.

From 2 December 1945, until late May 1946, the Division Jump School qualified 3,398 jumpers and made a total of 18,269 jumps. A world record was believed set when a single C-47 type aircraft jumped 735 men in one day.

In June 1946, the 11th Airborne Division Jump School moved to Yamoto Airstrip. At this time, it was designated "The Airborne School" and subsequently on 18 October 1946, was re-designated "The Airborne Training Center," 11th Airborne Division.

The mission of the Airborne Training Center is currently to qualify replacements as parachutists and the units of the Division as glider troops. To this end the school has qualified four battalions as gliderists and 14,000 men as qualified parachutists with a total of 110,000 parachute jumps.

The Airborne Training Center is at present under the command of Lt. Col. J. J. O'Kane."

Model C-82 Flying Boxcar

The army's ambitious plans for improving mobility was astonishing at the time. The following document, reproduced from a handout I received for the army demonstration event on May 12, 1947, describes the C-82's purpose and capabilities:

Model C-82 "Packet" – Cargo and Troop Carrier

"The C-82 "Packet," known to the Army as the flying boxcar because of its 2,916 cubic feet of cargo capacity, is now in production for the Army Air Forces.

Of all metal construction, the "Packet" is of the twin boom type, powered by two Pratt & Whitney double Wasp engines, each of which has 2100 horsepower available for take-off. A study has been made to determine the possibility of using the Pratt & Whitney 4360 engine in the "Packet."

Over one hundred C-82 "Packets" have been built for the Army Air Forces. Practically all of them have been assigned to the Ninth Air Force, now headquartered at Greenville Army Air Base, Greenville, South Carolina.

The 9ᵗʰ Air Force, which was formerly designated the 3ʳᵈ Air Force Troop Carrier, is in the process of converting from the C-47 and C-46 to the C-82. They are working out a completely new form of military strategy in which cargo aircraft will be used to transport a whole army to a given tactical position. Every item of equipment, with the exception of tanks, in the new Infantry Battalion Tables of Organization, will be designed for air transportation. Military freight can be loaded into the "Packet" through two rear doors which open up the entire rear of the cargo hold. Self-propelled vehicles can be loaded under their own power, thus avoiding the tactically expensive process of disassembly. All vehicles are ready for maneuvers as they roll from the plane.

A forward door increases the efficiency of personnel loading for airborne operations. Paratroopers can be dropped in two "sticks" from jump doors built into the larger cargo doors at the rear of the ship. Paratainers mounted on a monorail can be dropped through bomb bay doors simultaneously with the jumpers, thus permitting close grouping of personnel and equipment on the ground.

The tricycle landing gear provides a level cargo floor which simplifies loading and securing of cargo.

The C-82 "Packet" also serves as an ambulance airplane, carrying 34 litter patients and a glider tow craft. The Air Transport Command has used the "Packet" as a helicopter transport for Air-Sea rescue missions.

Military Specifications of the "Packet"

Span	106 feet, 5 inches
Overall length	77 feet, 1 inch
Overall Height	26 feet, 4 inches
Cargo Compartment Capacity	
(Unobstructed and continuous)	2,916 cubic feet
Wing Area	1,400 square feet
Gross Weight	
Provisional	50,000 pounds
Design	42,000 pounds
Empty Weight	28,000 pounds
Useful Load	22,000 pounds

Maximum payload for 500 miles   18,000 pounds

Maximum payload for 1000 miles   15,500 pounds

Maximum payload for 1500 miles   13,000 pounds

Crew

     Military   5

     Commercial   2

As Paratroop Carrier   42

As Ambulance   34 litters, 4 attendants

Landing Gear   Tricycle type, fully retractable

Construction   Aluminum alloy, fabric covered control surfaces

Performance

Cruising Speed   Over 200 miles per hour

Take-off run at sea level, loaded   800 feet

Service ceiling   25,000 feet

Single engine ceiling   8,000 feet

Maximum range   4,000 miles

Powerplant   2 Pratt & Whitney R-2800C twin row radial air-cooled engines with 2100 hp each at 2800 rpm for take-off, normal rating 1700 hp at 2600 rpm.

Note: All weight and performance figures are based on the results of preliminary flight tests conducted with full military equipment.

Most outstanding features of the "Packet" are:

     a)   Level floor at truck bed height – tricycle landing gear.

b) Square shaped interior with clear unobstructed space up and down, fore and aft.

c) High tail surface and utility of entire rear end of fuselage for loading and unloading.

d) Unusually short take-off distance, which enables it to use small strips and airports.

e) "Hot wing" anti-icing system, which can function on one or both engines. Tail group is heated in the same way by hot air ducts. Windshield anti-icing plus crew compartment and cargo hold temperature control are provided by this same system. "Packet" is first ship to enter production with such an anti-icing system.

f) Ability (height and width) to carry trucks, howitzers, half-tracks, etc.

g) Paratroop doors drop men in double time (door on each side) with no danger of striking tail and out of slip-stream.

h) Can be converted to hospital ship, carrying 34 litters, in less than 20 minutes."

HQ Staff

The following staff list is reproduced from a handout I received during a big show of capabilities on May 12, 1947, at our base.

HEADQUARTERS 11TH AIRBORNE DIVISION

Commanding General	Major Gen. Joseph M Swing
Chief of Staff	Lt. Col. D. P. Quandt
G-1	Lt. Col. L. L. Beckedorff
G-2	Major J. M. Kinzer
G-3	Lt. Col. J. P. Connor
G-4	Lt. Col. G. M. Barker
Adjutant General	Lt. Col. E. T. Henry

HEADQUARTERS 11TH AIRBORNE DIVISION REAR (SENDAI)

Assist. Div. Commander	Brig. Gen. William M Miley
Deputy Chief of Staff	Lt. Col. Richard J. Seitz
G-3 (Air)	Major Therwin S. Walters
G-4	Capt. C. C. Lumpkin
Adjutant General	CWO Harold R. Lloyd

Commanding General Division Artillery
Brig. General Edward McGaw
Commanding Officer 188th Parachute Infantry Regiment
Colonel R. Condon (Leave USA)
Acting Commanding Officer 188th Parachute Infantry Reg.
Lt. Col. E. H. La Flamme
Commanding Officer 511th Parachute Infantry Regiment
Lt. Col. E. H. Lahti
Commanding Officer 187th Para Glider Infantry Regiment
Colonel L. A. Riggins
Commanding Officer Division Special Troops
Lt. Col. N. E. Tipton
Commanding Officer Airborne Training Center
Lt. Col. M. J. O'Kane
Commanding Officer 152 Airborne Anti-Aircraft Battalion
Lt. Col. J. H. Farren
Commanding Officer 127th Airborne Engineer Battalion
Major R. C. Durgan
Division Parachute Officer
Major P. F. Lisk
Commanding Officer 11th Airborne Div. School Aeronautics
Major J. A. McCord

Telephone Directory

TELEPHONE NUMBERS

DIVISION HEADQUARTERS

Commanding General	Sapporo 6810
Chief of Staff	Sapporo 6812
G-1	Sapporo 6780, 6782
G-2	Sapporo 6783, 6784
G-3	Sapporo 6786, 6787
G-4	Sapporo 6793

DIVISION HEADQUARTERS REAR

Assistant Division Commander	Dial 206
Deputy Chief of Staff	Dial 213
G-3 (Air)	Dial 203, 214, 332
Parachute Maintenance	Dial 252
Motor Pool	Dial 267
188th Officers Club	Dial 468
Bar (Division Officers Club)	Loeper 136
Drop Zone	Glider Rear 172
Post Headquarters	Dial 306
Hospital	Dial 429

AIRBORNE SCHOOL

Commanding Officer	Carelus 6
Adjutant	Carelus 1
S-3	Carelus 3

40TH TROOP CARRIER SQUADRON

Commanding Officer	Carelus 5
Operations Officer	Carelus 25
Engineering Officer	Carelus 41

May 12, 1947 — One-sheet telephone "book"

Index

Made in the USA
San Bernardino, CA
31 December 2018